JUST TICKING

JUST TICKING THE BOX?

Refocusing School Attendance

Ben Whitney

© Ben Whitney, 2014

Published by Ben Whitney

A CIP catalogue record for this book is available from the British Library.

ISBN 978-0-9569568-4-2

Book layout and cover design by Clare Brayshaw

Prepared and printed by:

York Publishing Services Ltd
64 Hallfield Road
Layerthorpe
York YO31 7ZQ

Tel: 01904 431213

Website: www.yps-publishing.co.uk

CONTENTS

PREFACE

This book is an updated and substantially re-written version of '*A Guide to School Attendance*' published by David Fulton Books/ Routledge in 2008 (ISBN 978-0-415-46585-4). It is also a more detailed exploration of issues raised in Chapters 2 and 6 of my book, '*Social Inclusion in Schools: Improving Outcomes, Raising Standards*', David Fulton, 2007 (ISBN 978-1-843-12474-0).

As it has changed so frequently, I generally use the correct title for the relevant government department as it was at the time, i.e. DfEE, DfES, DCSF. For all current references, I use Department for Education (DfE), correct as from May 2010 in the hope that it will not have changed yet again by the time this book is published!

The views and opinions expressed are all entirely my own responsibility and do not necessarily reflect those of my previous employing local authorities, or any of their officers or schools.

Ben Whitney

ABOUT THE AUTHOR

Ben Whitney qualified as a social worker in the early 1970s. He then worked for several years in a local authority Children and Families Service before taking a postgraduate degree in Theology and spending over 10 years in church pastoral and community work. With the implementation of the Children Act 1989, he returned to local authority employment as a Specialist in Education Welfare. His work in helping schools to implement the implications of the Act led to the only book on the educational issues, first published in 1993: 'The Children Act and Schools'. He then spent 15 years in Staffordshire LA in a variety of senior roles before moving to be Team Leader for the Wolverhampton Education Welfare Service in 2004.

While in Wolverhampton he took a leading role in the West Midlands EWS Training Consortium which for several years delivered an NVQ qualification for EWOs. Throughout his career he has written and published widely including books for the Kogan Page 'Books for Teachers' series, contributions to the Croner Heads' Legal Guide and books for RoutlegeFalmer on social inclusion, child protection and school attendance.

Since retiring in 2011 Ben has worked for himself as an Independent Education Welfare Consultant and Trainer supporting and advising schools on pastoral care issues. He also delivers a regular series of seminars and has written email-based study programmes for FORUM Business Training on both attendance and child protection. He is a member of the Oaktree Co-operative, a group of current and former LA officers committed to promoting pupil welfare, safeguarding and wellbeing.

In addition to his professional work, he also writes on 'humanist spirituality' and can be contacted via his website: **www.ben-whitney. org.uk** which includes a regular blog on education and child welfare issues.

Also available from www.ben-whitney.org.uk

'HERE TODAY; HERE AGAIN TOMORROW'

Looking for a fresh approach to targeted work with KS2/3 pupils who need to improve their attendance? These newly-revised but tried and trusted materials give you everything you need to run a 4 x 30 minute groupwork programme which helps children (and their parents if possible) to understand their own absence and set personal targets for improvement.

£10 (no VAT)

'PREVENTING AND MANAGING ALLEGATIONS OF ABUSE ABOUT SCHOOL STAFF': A 'LEARN AND TRAIN' RESOURCE

Vanessa George, Nigel Leat, Jeremy Forrest etc. Is YOUR school safe from the risk of harm by someone in a 'position of trust'? Affects all sectors from nursery to FE. Many cases could have been avoided or detected earlier with a proactive approach that protects staff and children. 'An interesting programme that's really made me think. Thanks'.

- *3 self-study modules, each of approx 6000 words*
- *weblinks to key documents and resources*
- *questions for reflection*
- *activities and exercises*
- *model policies and procedures*
- *a final Power Point presentation with Notes*

PLUS the option of me delivering the Power Point at an interactive Seminar for your colleagues (at additional cost) if you prefer not to do this yourself.

£50 (no VAT)

INTRODUCTION

There are already many books about school attendance, absence and so-called 'truancy', so why yet another one? What makes this book different is that I begin with a radical question: 'Why do we bother'? Who, or what, is at the centre of our education system and therefore of all our efforts to make sure our current and future citizens make use of it? Attendance at school has never had a higher profile than it has today. Schools are awash with information now that computerised systems can do all the maths for us. Data is published for every school as part of the performance tables; thousands of parents are taken to court or have to pay Penalty Notice fines every year; endless meetings are held and home visits made to try and locate the missing. School staff and local authority (LA) officers spend hours and hours threatening, cajoling, bribing, encouraging and supporting children and young people to improve their attendance. No doubt all of them would really rather be somewhere else!

I am *not* saying that there is no point in any of this. Quite the reverse. It is essential that we do it. But I am asking *why* we do it and, crucially, is the way we spend our energies necessarily the best use of increasingly precious resources of time, money and skills? The law is there, I assume, for a purpose. And its purpose is.....? Not, I will argue, simply to create the data so that judgments can be made about the school; nor to 'crack down' on certain anti-social behaviours; nor to reinforce the authority of teachers or to give feckless parents a lesson on how they should be bringing up their children. These aims appear to dominate many people's thinking and drive most policies and practices, but I want to start somewhere else. My argument will be that is the *children* who should be at the centre. The law is not there to collect fines. Schools are not required to monitor attendance in order to satisfy Ofsted. Whatever we do in relation to school attendance and absence; indeed whatever we do in education as a whole, should have the children as the primary, or even as the only, focus. They are the 'customers'. The laws, guidance and procedures that provide the framework within which we all have to work are there to deliver the only meaningful outcome from all our efforts – what is best *for them*. And not just what is best for their intellectual and academic development but what is best for their whole lives, now and to come. And not just what is best for the majority but for all of them. It's an old-fashioned word, but it is every child's 'welfare' or wellbeing that matters, to them and ultimately to all of us. All of our thinking must keep that at the centre if what we do is to have any genuine value.

Monitoring attendance has certainly become more complex in recent years. It's not just about calling out names on a register twice a day, ticking the relevant box and waiting for the figures to be published. The mass of data that is now available has to be kept constantly under review and action taken in response to what it tells us. Otherwise it's just numbers that don't actually make any difference. But schools are changing. Increasingly they now have the power to vary their opening times and holidays from the traditional pattern. Afternoon registration amounts to 50% of the marks but might only account for 20% of the lessons. Children no longer necessarily have to be physically in the building to be learning, but they should still be in full-time supervised and outcome-based settings somewhere, not sat at home or just kept occupied to no apparent purpose. Despite the constant pressure for frequent testing and a more exam-driven culture, a new emphasis, at least here and there, on vocational subjects may yet turn some secondary schools in particular into quite different establishments whose older pupils may only be on the premises for two days a week but whose attendance still has to be closely monitored for all five. This all presents new challenges. But all schools, however they are governed and controlled, have to recognise that they have legal duties to manage their pupils' attendance as the regulations require, even if there is no longer an LA officer looking over their shoulder to check what they are doing. A school might easily avoid being rated 'inadequate', but are they actually meeting the needs of *all* their pupils? Their attendance records are supposed to be one way to make sure.

Fortunately, many school leaders accept that they need help in managing these wider responsibilities, at least some of the time. The importance of a range of professional expertise being available within the school, not just teaching staff, has been clearly recognised in recent years, even if those people do not always seem to get the salary and status that their expertise deserves. Many are former LA officers who have had to change employers to keep a job, or who have even become freelance workers no longer tied to an LA at all. I am hopeful that they will not lose their independent judgment and their whole-child emphasis as a result. The LA still has a statutory casework role to play *in extremis*, and must do it fairly and professionally. It may also be the commissioner of services and act as the school's 'critical friend' if invited to do so. But faced with the significant reductions in funding that will increasingly impact over the coming years, the LA will not offer the level of direct involvement with children and their parents that it used to. New kinds of 'service level agreements' and traded services are increasingly becoming the norm. The danger, however, is that vital pastoral tasks, including raising attendance, may then be no-one's main responsibility, just added onto the workloads of already busy people. The practical work of following up absences, contacting parents and making real use of the data, right down to the level of individual pupils, is normally best done by people other than teachers, but it requires specialist people to be recruited with the time to do it. And they need to keep the individual child constantly in mind, not be distracted by the school's overall performance priorities.

That may well involve sitting on the landing outside a child's bedroom for an hour or two waiting for them to speak to you, or remembering that it's their birthday today or doing 101 other things that don't feature in anyone's job description. I really don't expect a teacher to have time for all that. However, most classroom teachers will still supervise morning and afternoon registration and represent the school with parents and other agencies. They still spend more time with the children than anyone else and need to have a clear understanding of these wider issues in order to ensure they send out the right messages. Those who have been absent will need additional individual support once they return and help in catching up missed work. If we fail to meet their needs here, we may find ourselves with even greater disruption to their learning in future. Many staff, however, may be relatively unprepared for what they are expected to do. Despite the centrality of this role alongside their more formal teaching commitments, many will have received little specific training in these duties and will be almost entirely dependent on the extent to which the schools in which they work prepare them. Some will, as a result, learn bad habits alongside good ones!

ABOUT THIS BOOK

I hope this book will be of value to anyone who wants to approach issues of attendance and absence with a new perspective: school leaders, pastoral staff and governors, teachers in training and their tutors, newly-qualified teachers, school-based and LA Attendance and Welfare Officers, as well as those in other children's agencies who want to acquire a greater understanding of what goes on in education. It is not primarily a handbook on strategies for raising attendance, though there is a bit of that here and there, and some practical advice based on my own 25 years of experience of working with schools, especially in chapter 4. If you are looking for such a book, my old friend Emeritus Professor Ken Reid OBE has a wide range of excellent publications to meet this need: (e.g. 'An Essential Guide to Improving Attendance in Your School: Practical Resources for All School Managers', Routledge, October 2013).

Chapter 1 sets the scene after a brief look at our history. What then follows is essentially a personal commentary on current attendance and absence provision, looking at it from the specific angle of whether or not it enhances the pupils' welfare. This is the constant basis to my interest in attendance at all. Our systems are meant to have them as the focus; not schools, the state or even their parents. But there is still plenty of information about those systems here which I hope the reader will find helpful. Many people will never have actually read the regulations and guidance for themselves. You can trust me to do that accurately and to identify the key points for you. Then you can make your own mind up about whether or not I make a case for keeping the child at the centre in implementing them. Chapter 2 is primarily a reference guide to the relevant law and regulations, updated to reflect recent changes, before I then move on to consider the range of responsibilities undertaken by schools and LAs. (Different governance arrangements and legislation apply in each of England, Scotland, Wales and Northern Ireland. While written from an English perspective, the practical issues addressed in this book are essentially the same. Some key distinctions are noted in the text).

It is vital to recognise at the outset that the management of attendance and absence is not entirely a matter for individuals to act as they choose. The legal requirements create an overall environment within which schools', parents' *and* children's rights are all supposed to be maintained. It is, for example, as much an offence for the proprietor of a school to fail to operate in accordance with the regulations as it is for a parent to fail to fulfil their legal duty. Registers are legal evidence that must not be tampered with. This is not always acknowledged and one key aim of this book is to provide a convenient and comprehensive guide to the wide variety of expectations involved. These are to be found in several different places and would otherwise require extensive additional research by the reader. It is hoped that this information will lead to fewer mistakes, with the subsequent damaging consequences for everyone, caused either by ignorance of the law or a failure to see its implications.

The use of common registration categories, reinforced by the 2013 'DfE Advice', has been required from 2006/7, whatever computerised or manual marking system is used. These in particular are intended to lead to greater consistency in order to provide a fair basis for comparison between schools *and* to ensure that parents and children are not faced with different, conflicting or unreasonable expectations. But one school, or individuals within it, may still interpret their power to authorise absence more generously than another, thus totally changing the basis of whether a given absence is seen as a problem or whether there is any evidence against parents on which to proceed. So I will spend some time in chapter 3 outlining how the recommended codes are *supposed* to be used. Some discretion seems entirely appropriate, but how should it be exercised and in whose best interests? Schools vary widely in terms of their intake and may need quite different strategies according to local circumstances. Individual headteachers may create a particular ethos in how such matters are dealt with, but how can that process operate with fairness, not just with an eye to expediency?

However, while the legal framework is the same everywhere, the way in which it is interpreted will vary widely in practice, despite attempts by the DfE to introduce more standardised procedures. This makes it difficult to say precisely what 'should' happen in every case. For example, the fact that parents can be prosecuted when their children are not attending school 'regularly' requires several local definitions and decisions about whether or not it is the right thing to do in a particular case. Much will depend on the LA and inter-agency procedures that I discuss in chapter 5. There is, for example, no set level of absence that automatically results in legal action rather than some other response. So what should trigger it? In some LAs, schools will even issue Penalty Notice fines themselves or the enforcement criteria may be quite different from those used in a neighbouring area. But what drives this process, which agency should take the lead, and how are the appropriate actions selected?

This significant element of discretion means that much of this book is at the level of 'best practice' which may require some further work in the light of local circumstances. It takes full account of key resources from the government, and the Education Act 1996, the Children Act 1989 and the Education (Pupil Registration) (England) Regulations 2006 and subsequent amendments between

2010 and 2013. My intention is not simply to duplicate what these say but to develop their practical implications rather further than the official guidance and address real questions about their actual implementation. I try to refer to all the necessary documents and regulations at the appropriate place, but without inundating the text with references. This means an element of occasional repetition but it also avoids complicated cross-referencing that requires the reader to keep an eye on more than one chapter at once.

At various intervals in the text there are:

- summaries of key points or outlines of particular topics
- five longer articles which go into greater detail on one key area
- three 'Frequently Asked Questions' sections dealing with specific points of practice, together with
- three extended case studies in Chapter 6.

Throughout I try to maintain an approach based both on what can realistically be done in responding to absence in order to promote children's best interests *and* on what the law requires. I appreciate that this is sometimes a delicate balancing act between the interests of all the various parties involved. But in my view, far too many 'solutions' are advanced without first even asking what the 'problem' is. Equating all 'persistent absence' with 'truancy', for example, clearly doesn't cover it. That is grossly unfair on schools and on those who attend them. But I make no apology that the emphasis, at all times, is on those whose centrality is not always recognised in education: the children and young people who are entitled to receive it. We cannot measure our success by improvements in the data or by how many parents end up in the courts. We must measure it by whether our efforts make any genuine and lasting difference to children's lives, especially those who are on the margins. If we haven't got it right for them, every single one of them, then we haven't got it right, full stop.

CHAPTER 1

SETTING THE SCENE

GENERAL

I began the previous version of this book in 2008 by writing: 'Things are always on the move in education, not least in the pastoral care of children'. A few further years have removed none of this statement's accuracy. But are there some core principles that should never change? The Department for Education (DfE), (formerly the Department for Children, Schools and Families (DCSF), still oversees education, social work and family support services for children, though it is true to say that in the current government's educational agenda at least, school organisation, changes to the curriculum and examination reform appear to be by far the dominant concerns. 'Standards' are everything, which also seems to require ever-greater freedoms for schools to operate without external 'interference'. We have seen a rapid expansion in the number of academies and 'free schools', both of which effectively operate outside LA influence, (even if they still need the LA to co-ordinate their admissions). LAs have also lost many of their traditional support roles, and consequently many of their staff, though they continue to be responsible for the legal enforcement of attendance against parents; about the one thing left that only they can do, (at least for the time being). The Department's title, changed on virtually the first day of the new government, might give a misleading impression of what needs to be done. 'Education' does not operate in a vacuum. Engaging with both 'Children' and 'Families' is essential in order to get them to school to receive it.

At my previous time of writing, new local inter-agency collaborations in the provision of children's services were imminent. Most LAs now have much more co-ordinated teams, (though they are often also smaller in total than they used to be). 'Every Child Matters' and the National Behaviour and Attendance Strategy that supported LAs and schools in delivering it, have both come and gone, together with several other initiatives which had stressed the role of schools in local partnerships. There is now a greater emphasis on the individual school taking responsibility for dealing with its own priorities, if sometimes in new kinds of collaborations with other equally independent-minded schools. Many of the previous LA-level targets are no longer in place. 'Achieving' (without the 'Enjoying') is now the over-arching measure, rather than the previous government's emphasis on all the '5 outcomes' which took us well beyond the school gates. The White Paper that preceded the Education Act 2011 was called '*The Importance of Teaching*' which makes the priority clear. This is not to say that the Coalition has no interest in children's wider welfare, though it has also reduced some of the previous safeguarding and safer recruitment expectations and reversed some key elements of policy such as the establishment of the 'Contact Point' database, which would have met the constant call in Serious Case Reviews for professionals to communicate with each other more effectively.

But it sometimes looks as if education policies are somewhat out of step with other children's agencies where the emphasis is much more on finding 'joined-up' solutions to problems. There may yet be further changes in the light of the Munro Review of social work and the new arrangements for responding to Special Educational Needs and Disabilities (SEND), but schools are increasingly being encouraged to exercise greater autonomy and not necessarily to feel themselves bound by wider local inter-agency arrangements. Use of the Common Assessment Framework, for example, has often been seen as an unwelcome and somewhat optional burden. But children and families need a range of services to meet their needs; they do not become someone different when it comes to school. If there are issues of child protection or neglect, for example, which are often closely linked to chronic non-attendance, any suggestion that school staff should act alone in response would be deeply worrying. And of course, as cuts have begun to bite in LA budgets, many of the most vulnerable families and their children will be among those who will feel the loss of services most acutely. That will inevitably impact on their involvement in education.

Because of this overwhelming emphasis on schools, however, there has also been little political interest in the welfare of those children whose parents have chosen home education. For some it clearly works well. Most parents do a good enough job, within their own definition of what the job is. The Badman Review (2009) recommended much closer supervision of what they are required to provide, though it had no intention of denying them that right, which has always been there. But what kind of accountability is now appropriate? The initial context for the Review was the death of a child who was not in a school, but the underlying issue is to what extent the state should seek to regulate what parents provide and who has the right to inspect it. Neither of the two recent governments accepted the recommendation of compulsory registration of the arrangements with the relevant LA, so we still do not know how many such children there are or exactly what they are all doing all day. Schools *have* been reminded of the importance of following proper procedures if parents wish to withdraw their child to home educate them, but they cannot prevent them doing so and there is no requirement even to notify the LA that you or your children exist if you have never put them into a school in the first place.

This remains a significant loophole if the child's best interests are the driving concern. Even allowing for the relative rarity of actual abuse, I saw plenty of examples in my own casework experience of children who ended up socially isolated or engaged in a very limited 'educational' programme such as reading the Bible or caring for a younger sibling, whether or not this was what they wanted to do. Parental freedom, for some at least, has certainly won the day here. These parents, it seems, are to be entirely trusted to do what they know is best. This even includes a tolerance of so-called 'flexi-schooling' which, unlike for all other parents, allows them to send their child to a school only occasionally, perhaps just for science or music that they cannot provide themselves, provided they can reach an agreement to do so with the headteacher. (For some very small schools this might be a means of ensuring their survival as they are still funded as if the child were there full-time. It should result in very high levels of absence, but creative accounting sometimes seems to avoid this being the case). As I will explore later, this degree of flexibility might be entirely appropriate for some children. But whether this option is necessarily best for those whose parents and schools arrange it between themselves may be another question.

By contrast, 2012/13 saw several key changes, many of which have increased the power of schools and restricted parents' freedoms once your child becomes a 'registered pupil'. We know that being 'out of school' is a major contributor to social exclusion. But there is effectively no longer any right of appeal against your child being permanently excluded, only a limited opportunity to argue that the process was flawed. Even if an Independent Panel agrees that it was, they cannot overturn the governors' decision, only ask them to reconsider and extract a small financial penalty if they choose not to do so. Many children are simply 'sent home' or denied admission with no proper process at all. Parents are increasingly in the firing line, as critical comments by the Chief Inspector of Schools in October 2013 made evident. There is political pressure for more draconian interventions by social workers and for more children to be removed from 'inadequate' families and put up for adoption. At this point parents, or least some of them, have suddenly become the source of all society's ills, despite the requirements of the Children Act 1989 for agencies to work in partnership with them wherever possible.

As regards attendance in particular, the 2012 Report for the DfE by Charlie Taylor *Improving Attendance at School* signalled several changes that will be explored more fully later. Like others before him, he called for parents' Child Benefit to be removed if their children miss school, (which has not happened and almost certainly never will, except possibly post-16). But much of the general tone is also somewhat authoritarian and punitive. For example, the further restriction that he proposed on the authorising of holidays in term-time in 'exceptional' circumstances only, (which came into force from September 2013) seems popular with many headteachers and LAs. But it has proved very unpopular with many parents, including prompting an on-line petition with over 130,000 signatures. Fewer than 1 in 10 absences are accounted for by all holidays, authorised and unauthorised combined, (0.5% of all sessions), so is this issue really such a problem? The question at least deserves a hearing, just like the sometimes over-officious use of speeding cameras and parking fines. These laws are not actually meant to catch the driver who strays up to 33 mph for a few yards or who has just popped into a shop to get their dry-cleaning.

Similarly, educational penalties must be fair and proportionate, not jump on mere technicalities. Many parents feel they are now required to take a holiday at times when they can't afford it or to have no holiday at all. Not everyone has control over when their holidays are; shifts have to be shared out and services kept going. Of course there has to be some limit to the demand, but whether a short break with their parents might sometimes be to some children's benefit does not even seem to be up for discussion. Nothing is more important than being at school, except, of course, when an exclusion is appropriate, or it's an election day, or a review day, or a strike day, or it snows, etc. even if parents still have to go to work on those days. I suspect that many will still go on holiday anyway and risk the fine or lie and say their child was sick; then at least you don't get into trouble. But this issue in particular seems to be getting far more prominence than I personally feel it merits.

2013 also saw the issuing of the DfE's *Advice on School Attendance,* (4 versions in less than 8 months – the statutory and non-statutory elements are now in 2 different documents). These replaced all previous guidance to schools and LAs. They are remarkably short documents, in line with recent government practice, (at least in England; Welsh schools seem to need rather more support), and contain absolutely no information, case-studies or sharing of best practice about what works. They are all about responding to failure, not about celebrating success, despite the fact that, according to the published data at least, attendance has never been so good. I would like to have seen children, parents and schools given some credit for that improvement. But there is little or no advice on a welfare or strategic approach to dealing with absence, only a remorseless emphasis on enforcement. What the *'Advice'* does provide, in order to make sure that legal action is carried out appropriately, is considerable detail on how registration should be managed, including the correct code to be entered into the registers and the requirements regarding off-registration etc. That at least is welcome.

But the wider concern is whether there is much point in issuing such guidance at all. Do school leaders actually read it and then choose to follow it? (We will come back to the significance of this particular question several times later). There is increasingly limited opportunity for external supervision or inspection of what goes on day-to-day. Schools will be judged in part by how they mark their registers so of course there is a temptation to make things look as good as possible. The latest Ofsted Framework plays down the significance of attendance unless there are very serious and obvious weaknesses, focusing to a much greater extent on behaviour. LAs have no right to inspect the registers of schools they do not maintain, which is now a majority of secondary schools and a substantial percentage of primaries. Even where they can do so, given the massive reduction in Education Welfare Services in the last three years, there may be no-one left to do it: i.e. picking up poor registration practice, ensuring that individual children's needs are not being missed or that they are not disappearing from registers illegally. These are key safeguards to protect children which must not be overlooked.

However, if there is one thing that is still clear, it is that there is a correlation between attendance and achievement, at least for the vast majority of children whose absence is of the greatest concern. Those who attend best, generally achieve best, as we would hope. There are some who manage to buck the trend and we certainly do not want to send a signal that there is no point in bothering in the future if your attendance has been poor in the past. But raising attendance for those at greatest risk of missing out is not some separate, less important, 'soft' task than the core business of teaching and, vitally, learning. It is integral to them and, crucially, an issue that still has to be addressed if we are to have much hope of improving the outcomes for most of those who are currently on the margins. All that follows is an attempt to make sure we do not become distracted by the data and at their expense.

ABSENCE THEN AND NOW

A civilised society should always seek to learn from its past and if I were devising a system for genuinely universal education, I wouldn't personally start from here, largely because of what our history tells us. We have been concerned about those who do not take part with much enthusiasm ever since schools as we know them were created. If everyone had signed up for the education available, compulsion would never have been necessary, but it has always been part of our modern system. Some people have never wanted what schools have to offer. What might we reasonably have learnt about them as a result by now? Our modern British story begins about 1816 when the Parliamentary Committee on the 'Education of the Lower Orders' first drew attention to the fact that the 'poor of all descriptions' did not currently have access to any structured education. Up to that point it was largely the preserve of the wealthy, usually only for boys, and other parents were just expected to do the best they could themselves, alongside, of course, their children's own working lives.

So there was a tremendous drive to get more schools established. Some of our current buildings, especially some rural primary schools, still date back to not long after this era. But there was a problem:

> 'A very important part of the population we cannot touch at all; I refer to the most degraded of the poor. The children of trampers and beggards. Sometimes, by extraordinary efforts, we get some of these children into school, but they are off again almost immediately; and

those are the children from whom a very large proportion of our prisons are peopled. Now the difficulty is, how to get these children under instruction and how to keep them (there).

(Evidence to the Parliamentary Report on the State of Education, 1834).

There has long been a recognition that not everyone would necessarily want to receive the education being made available, especially those whose general lifestyle did not conform to what the growing middle classes expected. The 'upper orders' of course still opted to make their own arrangements because many of those employed by the emerging School Boards were of dubious character and limited education themselves. You only have to read Dickens to get a sense of it. Thousands of parents still make that choice and educate their children themselves because they don't necessarily see school as a positive place for them to be. But poorer and less educated parents, then as now, were expected to conform to what was on offer and be grateful. Clearly, not everyone was!

The model eventually adopted, especially for secondary education, was essentially borrowed from the elite 'public' (i.e. private) schools already in place. It was not a new one devised for its more universal purpose. Much of what we normally define as inherent in a 'good' school today would be instantly recognisable by our better-educated Victorian forebears. As I will argue later, this still risks leaving the 'trampers and beggards' on the sidelines. They know that schools like these aren't really for them because all their day-to-day experience continues to emphasise how marginalised they are. The early reformers saw the only answer as compulsion and we are still stuck into the same mentality – 'it's good for you so take your medicine'. If the undeserving poor didn't want to go voluntarily then education would have to be enforced. It was that or the workhouse.

By the Newcastle Report of 1861, all but 'about 100,000' of the estimated 2 million children of the poor were in schools of some kind, at least part-time up until the age of 11. But the available schools were often still of very limited quality and few children remained there beyond 13. By contrast, there were only 320,000 children in total who were reckoned not to belong to the poorer classes and there were those who argued that extending educational entitlement to so many children was a mistake:

'Even if it were possible, I doubt whether it would be desirable with a view to the interests of the peasant boy, to keep him at school till he was 14 or 15 years of age. But it is not possible. We must make up our minds to see the last of him, so far as the school day is concerned, at 10 or 11'.

(Evidence to the Newcastle Report by Revd. James Fraser, later Bishop of Manchester).

That sounds like a cunning plan to avoid them staying away! But others raised more self-analytical and philosophical questions. Matthew Arnold, one of the Newcastle Commissioners who went around the country seeing what was in place, argued in a Report of 1867 that there was something about the British way of life that valued education less highly than they did, for example, in Prussia (Germany). Education, he argued, flourishes there not because it is compulsory, but because the people wanted it:

'Because people there really prize instruction and culture, and prefer them to other things, therefore they have no difficulty in imposing on themselves the rule to get instruction and culture. In this country people prefer....politics, station, business, money-making, pleasure and many other things; and till we cease to prefer these things a law... cannot be relied upon to hold its ground and to work effectively'.

This strikes me as amazingly up-to-date in its analysis. Maybe a small minority of people are still more impressed by other sources of self-advancement than by what happens in our schools. I imagine that Matthew Arnold would have some very sharp comments to make about our modern obsession with 'reality' TV and the activities of sport stars and celebrities, but he would probably also recognise that there are many ways to make money in our culture and not all of them require the sorts of qualifications envisaged by Michael Gove! We might not entirely approve of these attitudes but there is no point in pretending they don't still exist.

The 1870 Education Act was designed to deal with all these uncertainties and to set a standard for compulsory education, at least up until the age of 12. The legal sanctions now being used that I will discuss in Chapter 2 still date from this pioneering legislation. The parental defences against prosecution for non-attendance defined in the 1870 Act are almost identical to those in force today. Other forms of education were still legal, but were in practice available only to those who could pay for them. School was for the masses, whether they liked it or not. And still not everybody went, or at least not willingly. Education Welfare Officers look back with some affection to a Mr William King, appointed by the Council of the Reformatory and Refuge Union in 1865 as its first Attendance Officer. Interestingly, his job description suggests that not only force was involved, (though he almost certainly carried a very big stick), but his work included tasks such as 'providing immediate shelter and food'. By the 1876 Education Act attention had to be paid to financial support if children were to attend and, by 1906, free meals. We will often come back to this more welfare-based approach later.

The Balfour Education Act of 1902 extended the period of compulsory education, (raised again to age 14 in 1918) and the responsibility passed from the unelected School Boards to the emerging LAs. (It is now passing back again!) In a little-remembered series of 'strikes' just over 100 years ago, working-class pupils in urban communities all over the country walked out of school in protest at the harsh conditions and in support of their disadvantaged parents. Many were publically beaten or sent to the workhouse as a result. The idea that there might actually be something wrong with what they were being offered probably never occurred to the educational establishment. In my view we are still in danger of laying all the blame at the feet of those who choose not to participate and drifting into increasingly simplistic responses that will take us nowhere.

By the 1930s questions were again being raised about the value of much that was being offered. The last sentence of this quotation from the Report of the Consultative Committee on Primary Education (1931) reads as if it has been written by an Ofsted inspector:

'No good can come from teaching children things that have no immediate value for them.... to put the point in a more concrete way, we must recognise the uselessness and the danger of seeking to inculcate..inert ideas – that is, ideas which at the time they are imparted have no bearing upon a child's natural activities of body or mind and do nothing to guide or illuminate his experience....While there is plenty of teaching which is good in the abstract, there is too little which helps children directly to strengthen and enlarge their instinctive hold on the conditions of life by enriching, illuminating and giving point to their growing experience.'

No wonder they didn't go! Not all teaching is good enough today or necessarily relevant according to inspection reports and the DfE, but the children are still expected to be there. The landmark 1944 Butler Act was yet again supposed to put everything right by ensuring that every child was educated according to (his) 'age, ability and aptitude'. ('Special educational needs' was not added until much later). But the range of schools envisaged never actually materialised in many places, especially the technical schools. In practice we ended up with a two tier system: selective grammar schools for the clever ones and secondary moderns for all the rest. I still remember my contemporaries in the top year at primary school being told that they hadn't 'failed' the 11

Plus; they'd just been 'selected' for the secondary modern school. I doubt they saw it that way. I was secretly rather disappointed that I had been 'selected' for the all-boys grammar school, though I suppose I shouldn't have been. I was one of the lucky ones.

With the raising of the school leaving age to 16, many new initiatives had to be introduced to keep the ROSLA children on board. That was my father's job for a while and I distinctly remember him saying that it was like trying to hold sand in your fingers. Various Reports drew attention to the fact that so many children had little to show for their years of schooling, but the emphasis was increasingly on the duty on parents to make sure their children went and not much on asking ourselves why some didn't. Many parents still feel they have little or no power over the provision available. Like their C19th peers, their commitment and that of their children, may therefore be similarly limited. Despite all the talk of 'choice', they know that it is mostly schools who do the choosing and their children may end up in one that was their 3rd or 4th 'preference'. This lack of personal investment in the system was not such a big problem in the past when there was ample unskilled, if generally available work at the end. For a significant number, school was just what you did until you were old enough to leave and they just put up with it. But failure at school can now mean failure for life.

Thankfully we no longer send children with severe learning disabilities to distant hospitals and rural 'colonies'. (Visiting them was part of my job as a social worker as late as the 1970s). But there is certainly a small, if largely hidden, illegal juvenile workforce that still exists at the margins and keeps some older children from participating in education as they should. Some children are too sick, physically and emotionally, to be in school, (though, if so, there is a statutory duty to meet their needs in other ways). Some are too damaged by abuse and neglect to attend at present, including some who are living within the care system. Not all children, including some who have arrived from overseas or live in communities that travel, are known to the authorities or are on shared databases. Many 'disappear' from schools during Key Stage 4 or soon afterwards. Other children, like Victoria Climbié, (whose murder led to the Laming Report in 2003 and a major national review of child safeguarding procedures), or Khyra Ishaq (whose death did not result in any significant change at all), are deliberately kept from the education system by parents or carers who may pose a significant risk to their health and welfare.

Some parents still can't quite see why we are making so much fuss, or, because of issues arising from their mental health or other family problems, do not see the need to do anything about their child's absences from school. Some children are caring for their parents or other family members in school-time or have become disaffected from the whole system. Some are at home because there is no place for them or because we cannot manage their behaviour or meet their learning needs. They may have no school from which to stay away. All this we know. Schools are still far from universal. If every child is our focus, we must continue to look well beyond them.

CURRENT TRENDS

Despite all the recent concerns about 'truancy', 'unauthorised absence' (the correct term), remains extremely low overall. It is in challenging explanations for absence, previously seen as acceptable, or through additional support for the schools facing the greatest challenges, that most progress may have been made, statistically at least. Nationally, there is a mixed picture about school attendance and media headlines often give a misleading impression. Overall attendance is certainly higher than it was, but it is also true that a significant reduction in unauthorised absence has not been achieved since the current system began. In 2005/6, for example, it was 1.2% of all sessions in England, 1.7% in Wales and 1.8% in Scotland, and considerably higher than that in some individual schools. It fell to around 1% on average in England several years ago and has more or less stayed there although there has been a very slight increase again recently. (It is still higher in the other regions). But this may be accounted for by most schools becoming more strict in their expectations and implementing the regulations more rigorously. Rising unauthorised absence does not necessarily mean more absence; only the re-classification of more of the existing absence as unacceptable.

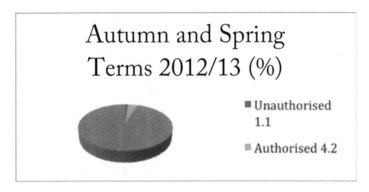

Autumn and Spring Terms 2012/13 (%)

- Unauthorised 1.1
- Authorised 4.2

The definition of a 'persistent absentee' has changed from under 80% attendance to under 85%, so of course there are now more of them, though the general trend is downwards, especially in secondary schools. Average overall attendance still goes up and down a little, primarily due to factors such as the extent of winter flu, as illness accounts for the overwhelming majority of absences (over 3% of total sessions). 2011/12 was a particularly good year for levels of sickness; 2012/13 was not so good. The published figures clearly reflect this difference, over which schools (and perhaps even most parents) have little or no control. There is now a much greater emphasis on reducing overall absence, and not so much on the distinction between whether absences are authorised or unauthorised. A few schools, however, still seem to see keeping unauthorised absence low, or even non-existent, as the key target and may therefore simply authorise more generously. The amount of overall absence may be just the same either way.

There appears to be a 'hardcore' of about 2-5% of pupils (and/or their parents), for whom nothing much works and who are seriously disengaged from education, about the same percentage as those who were reckoned to have opted out of the provision in the C19th. Watch the film 'The Selfish Giant' if you want to get a feel for the kinds of lives they lead. These are largely the same children that the government's 'Troubled Families' programme has recognised as being outside most mainstream services, not only education. Despite this obvious need for integrated approaches, the DfE '*Advice*' still seems to assume that only prosecutions are required, with just a token nod to other kinds of interventions. Most of these children will be among those classed by the media as 'persistent truants', though a complex range of reasons for their absence may be involved. I was often expected to 'do something' about such families when I worked for an LA, despite the fact that many had no school, or all their absences had been authorised and sometimes their school had even initiated them. That just illustrates how muddled so much of our thinking is.

This small group account for most of the serious absence but they are not evenly distributed. Some schools have many more of them than others. The sad truth is that in an increasingly competitive climate nobody really wants them and I probably wouldn't go either if I were in their shoes. We will keep coming back to them to make sure that they are not forgotten. But this still means that about 99% of the time children are either in school or only ever absent with the school's agreement. Without minimising the problems, especially for those who are effectively 'lost', this does not entirely match the picture of widespread anti-social attitudes sometimes portrayed by politicians of all persuasions. We are actually doing pretty well; it's a pity the DfE rarely recognises it.

All school staff across all Key Stages are involved in these responsibilities, even those working in Early Years. But while the attendance of these younger children in Reception year is now being monitored through the Census, it is not currently part of each school's published data. National figures published so far suggest about 6% of sessions are lost to absence at this stage but I'm not sure what this tells us as schools may have been recording the figures differently. The attendance of these children is not necessarily compulsory so were the missing sessions classed as 'absence' or just discounted? This uncertainly must make the figures unreliable. Staff must appreciate the distinction in order to avoid challenging parents without legal authority to do so. Of course good habits established here can only benefit the child later. But parents do have a genuine choice for once and some will feel their child is not ready for full-time school until the specified date. They have every right to make that decision, or to take a break from school whenever they want to without criticism. If we now expect their children to be there then we should change the age of compulsion.

When it comes to pupils who *are* of compulsory school age, the government has placed extensive legal obligations on all schools in addition to the need to deal appropriately with individual cases:

- recording, reporting and publishing information about absence and attendance;
- a duty to take twice-daily attendance registers, using suggested codes and categories (or their equivalent without the freedom to change their statistical meaning);
- annual absence target-setting;
- notifying data to the DfE, (each term and annually, now for all 6 half-terms not 5 as before);
- providing attendance information for parents;
- notifying the LA when children are removed from the admission register or have not attended without explanation for 2 weeks;
- assisting in legal action where required.

Sticks or carrots?

Critics might suggest that if our schools were good enough, or perhaps if education were not free, everyone would want their children to be there and they would queue up to go! That certainly seems to be the experience of countries in the developing world where provision is scarce and costly, though there too there are those on the margins who choose to opt out. Some element of legal enforcement has always been retained, and, along with it, the existence of the 'School Board

---

Man' (sic) and their contemporary LA equivalent in order to chase up the reluctant. An elderly acquaintance of mine remembers a man known as 'Daddy Whitney', (no relation as far as I am aware), who terrorised the children of Crewe in the late 1930s! Penalties, fines and even imprisonment are still an essential part of our system and are still used extensively with virtually no change to the law in 150 years.

However, some would argue that if real progress is to be made, reforms of current structures, specifically designed to place the learning needs of individual children at the centre, might be more effective, including opportunities that look very different from the current emphasis on 'schools'. Perhaps older children even ought to be paid for attending in order to promote an appropriate work ethic in return, as with adults. 'What's in it for me'? has become a question that previous generations might not have considered important, but in today's consumer culture is crucial. People rarely become more positive about education by force. Incentives and positive reinforcement may now be needed, not just sanctions that are unlikely to provide the necessary motivation on their own.

Despite what is arguably quite an impressive level of attendance overall, individual schools are clearly expected to do more to promote it than used to be the case. These levels have not been achieved by accident. School policies are essential for establishing good practice in promoting as high a level of attendance as possible and are in everyone's best interests. There is a 'model' policy later in this book that could be used as starting-point if your school needs to review its current arrangements. Addressing the issues in an open and pro-active way is likely to prevent greater problems occurring further on in the child's educational career *and* make sure that children's needs are identified and met. Even if this does not benefit your own school then perhaps it will help your colleagues later. The earlier the intervention, the better it will be for everyone in the long run.

There are, perhaps, more opportunities not to attend school nowadays than there ever used to be: the Internet, 500 TV channels all day, year-round theme parks, longer paid holidays, relatively cheap foreign travel, parents out at work etc. Staying at home has never been easier or more attractive. Perhaps this range of alternatives makes the levels of attendance now being achieved even more impressive. An element of inevitable teenage rebellion makes even the most ordered and functional family vulnerable to occasional unauthorised absences. So even the most stimulating and well-organised school needs to be aware of what may need to be done to ensure that all their pupils attend as they should. It is entirely 'normal' for a child or young person to test the boundaries and see what happens if they do not fall in with what is expected of them all the time. Such behaviour is not necessarily an indicator of major family problems or evidence of a developing anti-authority attitude in either child or parent.

Some children just skip school occasionally to do something else, perhaps showing an entirely natural avoidance of something difficult or less than exciting, without necessarily repeating the behaviour over again. Many adults do the same if they can get away with it! Some parents have what they see as more urgent priorities to deal with today and school just has to wait till tomorrow. Bullying, including by text and in social media, is certainly a significant factor. Teenagers frequently fall out with each other and with being together all day. Much use of attendance and absence procedures is just a routine pastoral response and many situations are capable of relatively easy resolution through prompt action by school staff and parents. There is no need for moral panic. However, in some cases of non-attendance, perhaps an increasing number, not being at school is only the presenting problem betraying something much greater underneath. There are many vulnerable children who cannot be expected to attend school while all else crumbles in chaos around them. These include:

- those whose families are in crisis;
- those experimenting with sex, drugs, alcohol or other abusive substances;

- those caught up in crime and gangs;

- those with major mental health needs;

- many children in the public care system;

- the victims of abuse and of discrimination;

- those grappling with the implications of caring for their parents or siblings;

- those affected by homelessness, poverty, domestic violence and wider 'social exclusion'.

There are certainly some parents who do not seem to care about the effect that missing school may have on their children in the long run, but I always want to ask 'why?' and they are far from typical of all those whose children are sometimes absent. Assessing the *reason* for the absence is crucial rather than jumping to any particular conclusion too quickly. The law seeks to be realistic in recognising that 100% attendance is not necessarily required, allowing for 'sickness and other unavoidable cause' which can justify the child being absent. Some situations are given special recognition of the fact that regular school attendance may not be practicable. Other children may also be allowed to have as much time off school as they need to take part in professional modelling, sport, films, stage shows and TV programmes etc. which may have to be done during the day. This makes an interesting contrast with the pressure on parents not to take their children on holiday in term-time just because the prices are cheaper then or to keep them off school with minor illnesses. 'Part time' attendance, agreed with the school, is not at all uncommon, especially for some older pupils or those with challenging behaviour. Education can take place away from the actual building in other settings or, increasingly, by means of information technology and distance learning, as well as by traditional methods.

This flexibility can all be a helpful way of 'differentiating' provision for those who need something out of the ordinary to meet their needs. But it can also be a way of putting the young person out of sight and out of mind. Being known to a school, and monitored on a *daily* basis, is meant to be a significant contribution to ensuring a child's general welfare. If they are not required to be there, what other provision needs to be in place to keep them safe? The detailed laws and regulations are there, at least in part, in order to protect them. Both parents and professionals are therefore required to follow them. Effective management of attendance and absence is not only about the cold enforcement of regulations, but simple justice suggests that there should be some consistency to avoid any suggestion that certain children and families have been subject to sanctions on an arbitrary or prejudicial basis while others have been allowed to be absent. In my experience, the legal basis of the judgments that are made by school staff and LA attendance professionals is not always as clear, consistent and impartial as it surely should be. The law can be both tender and tough but it should not be unjust, discriminatory or ignored just because its implementation raises difficult questions. So what is it able to do and how should it best be used?

CHAPTER 2

THE LEGAL FRAMEWORK FOR ATTENDANCE

EDUCATION ACT 1996

This outlines the basic legal obligations on parents and replaced the relevant sections of the Education Act 1944 and the Education Act 1993 from November 1st 1996.

Duty on parents

S.7 of the Education Act 1996 says, *'the parent of every child of compulsory school age shall cause him to receive efficient full-time education suitable–*

(a) to his age ability and aptitude and

(b) to any special educational needs he may have,

either by regular attendance at school or otherwise.'

'Registered' or 'Otherwise'?

Whether or not a child is a 'registered pupil' at a school is a crucial issue that is explored in detail below. This definition is of fundamental importance in knowing what may be reasonably expected of a parent. The right to educate their child 'otherwise' than at school if they wish to, has always been a principle of our system. If parents opt to educate their children themselves, they do not have to deliver the National Curriculum, nor spend a given number of hours in formal instruction, provided the education is 'suitable' to the child's needs. Court judgments in the past have suggested that the only

---

> *test is whether the child is adequately prepared for adult life in the community of which they are a member, not necessarily whether they reach a standard of academic attainment that might be seen as the norm within the schools. (Pupils with a Statement of SEN may be subject to rather greater scrutiny and the LA may have a right to intervene more robustly).*
>
> *True empowerment of parents may be about exploring perfectly legal alternatives, but, while their child is a registered pupil, a whole series of obligations apply. Changing this status, whether the initiative is taken by the parent or the school, is of enormous significance. The focus of this book is on those who make use of schools, but this wider context must always be remembered, especially where any question arises about removing children from the admission register, including permanent exclusion and alternative educational programmes.*

It is assumed for legal purposes that any educational programme provided through a school or an LA, including any supervised tuition delivered at home or elsewhere, will meet the necessary criteria. Such provision should be 'full time' unless the circumstances are exceptional. But a number of key words are not defined in more detail. What is required for an education to be 'efficient' or 'suitable'? What has to be provided 'otherwise'? These can all be a matter of some dispute. If parents take up the 'otherwise' option by providing the education themselves, (and at their own expense), the degree of scrutiny may be very limited. Officers have no right of entry to people's homes or to see the child studying. Parents do not actually have to produce evidence of work or written timetables for inspection, though many do so voluntarily. Many also access help and advice that may be available to support them. But it is up to the LA to prove that the parent is *not* educating the child if they are not satisfied with the arrangements, not the other way round. Home-educating parents may choose to enrol their child at a Further Education college from age 14, may organise themselves into alternative teaching groups, or can always choose to return their child to a school at a later date.

Education Act 1996: SUMMARY

Duty on parents

Parents have a legal duty to ensure that their children of compulsory school age are 'properly educated, either at school or otherwise', according to their 'age, ability, aptitude and any special educational need' (s.7)

Definition of compulsory school age

Children between the beginning of the term after they become 5 and the end of the school year in which they become 16 (the last Friday in June for all pupils) (s.8). (The 'expectation of participation' beyond Year 11 is just that, not a legally-enforceable requirement on either the parent or the young person).

School Attendance Order

An Order issued by an LA which requires a parent to register their child at a school (s.443) and therefore become a 'registered pupil'. A court can fine the parent if they do not comply.

Prosecution of parents

Where a 'registered pupil' fails to attend 'regularly', s.444(1); the enhanced offence', s.444(1A) (as amended by the Criminal Justice and Court Services Act 2000) and s.444(ZA) which allows prosecution of parents where children fail to attend alternative provision (Education Act 2005 s.116)

Registered pupils

Once a parent chooses to register their child of compulsory school age at a maintained or an independent school, (which includes academies and 'free schools'), the child must then attend 'regularly'. A child who comes to school only every Monday might be said to be attending 'regularly', but they are clearly also falling foul of the requirement to receive an education 'full-time'. In effect this means that any session (half day) on which the child is absent without the defence criteria being met (see below), can be evidence of an offence. The number of offences needed to justify a legal or even a more pastoral response, is, however, not defined in law. It is important to note that the obligation still falls entirely on the *parent*, not on the child. Children are not legally responsible for their own attendance and so far, at least, there has been no transfer of responsibility with the increase in the 'participation' age. 'Truancy' is not an offence like shoplifting. It is absence condoned by parents, or, indeed, about which they are powerless but for which they still have to be held legally accountable, which is the sole focus of any enforcement, right up to the end of June in Year 11. This is often overlooked or language such as 'taking the child to court' may be used. This is inaccurate and potentially counter-productive. Whatever sanctions may be appropriate in response to a child's poor attendance at school, the law currently allows no action in the courts against them, only against their parents.

This suggests that any legal proceedings are supposed to be taken in the child's best interests. The LA's actions should be solely intended to ensure improved outcomes for them, not to seek retrospective punishments that will make no difference. If that is not the likely outcome; if previous prosecutions have not resulted in improving their attendance, for example, I just do not understand why some LAs prosecute the same parent 3 or 4 times, each time to no effect. In times of scare provision, this strikes me as utterly pointless and we will come back later to some more meaningful alternatives. But that's the way the law is designed and it's important that everyone understands it correctly. It is intended *only* for situations of deliberate parental failure, nothing else. While the suggestion has often been made that 'truancy' should be made an offence by the child, the rhetoric has always given way once the problems of definition have been encountered. This is not to say that missing school may not be a risk factor in care proceedings or an issue in a youth justice setting, but it is not, in itself an activity for which a child can be 'punished' through the courts.

'When can I leave school'?

This changed from 1998, when a single leaving date for all children in the relevant year group was introduced: (Education (School Leaving Date) Order 1997). All those who are 16 on or after 1st September and are therefore in that year's Year 11, can currently leave school on the following last Friday in June, but not before. The 'raising of the school-leaving age' to 18 by 2015 (as it is sometimes described) is not that at all. No further extension of the legal requirements on parents is involved, only an 'expectation' that all those up to 18 will be in either some kind of further education, not necessarily full-time, or receive on the job training, rather than being paid benefits. It was originally proposed that there would be some legal sanction against young people, parents or employers if they did not take up the offer but all these ideas were found to be unworkable on further reflection.

It is worth mentioning here that the leaving date also relates to the law regarding part-time work by children. Although it is widely ignored, it is intended to protect children's health, safety and welfare up until the point they become 'young people'. Any work in a 'commercial enterprise', paid or unpaid, is illegal before this date unless the LA has issued a child-specific licence to the employer. The hours that can be worked and the kinds of work that can be done are all very tightly defined – but nobody takes much notice! I fully accept that the law is in desperate need of modernisation – parts of it are 90 years old. But here is another example of how the welfare of children seems to be of less political significance than the needs of employers for cheap labour (below the minimum wage) coupled with the desire of children themselves to seek an independence which, as in other areas, may lead them into wholly inappropriate settings. Quite why successive governments of all persuasions have never found time to address this issue is intriguing, given their constant tinkering with so many other elements of children's lives.

Many parents and employers, (let alone the pupils), appear to believe that the obligation to educate ends on the child's 16th birthday. I have even heard social workers say the same as, oddly, you can 'leave care' then even if you still have 9 months of compulsory education remaining. This has never been the case in England and Wales, though Scotland is different. Even when there were Easter and May leavers, the 16th birthday only determined which of these two dates was significant. This rule applies to every child in the relevant age cohort, including those educated outside the school system. All pupils, even those who may not be taking GCSEs, should still receive a full-time educational programme right up to the leaving date. (The DfE may in due course collect Y11 attendance data right up to the end of June, not just to the end of May as at present. Quite rightly that would raise some interesting issues for many schools if they are not all to become 'persistent absentees'!) They do not necessarily have to be present at school all the time but should not be allowed simply to stay at home on 'study leave' when they have nothing for which to study. They cannot begin work or move into post-16 settings before the end of June. (Those with birthdays in July or August will still be 15 and may have to wait till then). There is no legal reason why a parent cannot be prosecuted for failing to ensure their child is educated, even if he/she is already 16, if they have not yet reached the leaving date. But there must obviously be some purpose to such action rather than simply bolting the stable door long after the horse has disappeared over the horizon!

School Attendance Orders

School Attendance Orders (Education Act 1996 s.437- s.443) are for use only where children of compulsory school age are not registered at a school, but the LA takes the view that they should be. They are more properly described as 'School Registration Orders' and have no relevance in the context of a child who is already a registered pupil but who is not attending. They can be a difficult resource to use, especially where the child would pose any admitting school difficulty in managing their behaviour or learning needs. There is a long and complicated procedure for giving parents various options first and a series of formal letters and Notices must be served within defined timescales. They are used primarily where children have not been registered at age 5 or on secondary transfer or where the home education allegedly provided by parents has been judged inadequate.

SAO procedures

Parents must first reply to a letter indicating whether they are educating their child 'otherwise'. If they do not enrol their child at this point, if they do not reply, or if the LA does not accept the parent's explanation, the parent must then be written to again to explain that the child should be registered at a school. The parent is invited to choose a school (at which a place must be available) or the LA may nominate its choice of school.

Most parents who get this far then register their child at one of the schools in response and the process ends. Others may move away from the area at this point or provide the information that was asked for in the first place. If they do not respond within 15 days, the LA may serve the Order itself, naming the required school. If the parent still does not act to register the child at this point, they are committing an offence and can be prosecuted. The problem is that even if they are then fined, the child still isn't in school and no-one is quite sure what should happen next beyond doing it all over again! Once served, the Order remains in force for any subsequent school unless it is discharged. SAOs are rare but not unknown.

At its worst, this procedure can become very drawn-out with much potential for dispute about whether the parent has genuinely tried to get the child into a school, and potential issues about whether a suitable school is available. The difficulty of making a parent re-admit their child to a school once he/she is no longer a registered pupil makes it essential that pupils are not removed from a school's

---

admission register without a great deal of caution. A parent cannot be held accountable for the fact that a child is not attending once he or she is no longer a registered pupil. Some of these situations can then drag on for long periods without resolution during which time the child may be receiving no education at all, if either parents or schools act without proper regard to the regulations (see below).

Prosecution of parents (s.444(1) and s.444(ZA))

Parents commit an offence if a registered pupil does not attend 'regularly'. The definition of 'parent' includes *any* adult living with and looking after the child, even if they are not actually related, including foster-carers, (though not staff from public agencies). Those with 'parental responsibility' under the Children Act 1989 but who live apart from the child, can lawfully be prosecuted but this is rare unless they are actively undermining efforts to improve the child's attendance. LAs can only prosecute on the basis of *unauthorised* absence (see below and chapter 3 for the significance of this for registration practice). Enforcement is the responsibility of the LA where the school is, (not the authority in which the child lives if this is different). Legal action can also be taken where registered pupils are absent from Pupil Referral Units or failing to attend alternative provision without good reason.

Although the maximum fine under s.444(1) is £1000, most fines are much lower and Courts must take some account of the parents' ability to pay. They may fine the maximum if the parent does not appear in person, at least to begin with. Many cases are dealt with by means of small weekly or monthly payments, a conditional discharge or penalties such as a Community Rehabilitation Order. A greater range of outcomes is now available to the court as a result of the Crime and Disorder Act 1998, including the use of a Parenting Order. This Order places the parent under an obligation to work with the LA, school or a member of the Youth Offending Team to address the question of their attendance, as a means of reducing the likelihood that the child may go on to commit criminal offences in future. However, provision for parenting support is patchy and as there is still no offence by the child, their inclusion in 'youth offending' procedures at this point is a little confusing. This longer-term intervention following up the Court appearance for several further months has been seen, in many cases as replacing the need for Education Supervision Orders under the Children Act 1989, (though I would still argue for their continued usefulness, see below and chapter 5).

Providing the evidence

It is the school's attendance register that provides the evidence on which the parent is convicted. Registers are legal documents, which is why they must be kept strictly in accordance with the regulations, (Education Act 1996 s.434(6)). Headteachers may be required to account to the Court for any discrepancies or mistakes. A claim that they are accurate, when they are not, would be perjury. Any dispute between the parent and the LA about whether, for example, a given absence should have been authorised, will require the personal evidence of the headteacher in explaining the criteria used. It is the school's decision. This is why schools must have written and consistently-applied attendance policies and authorisation criteria that enable parents to know what the rules are and to ensure good practice by staff.

The LA will usually manage the prosecution process through a 'fast-track' procedure, designed to identify those parents where this action is most likely to be effective: 'Is prosecution the best available tool for the job?', not 'We'll have to prosecute because we can't think of anything else'! This will often mean that not all unauthorised absences can be proceeded with. That would be both unrealistic and, in many cases, unjust, but the criteria should be clear to everyone. Given the significant reduction in LA support in recent years, this may be the *only* role that they play in this context, (and they cannot charge schools for it). So it is essential that there is a clear local agreement about where the 'threshold' is and an effective process of making referrals so that those cases that have already reached a point where legal action may be needed are not left unresolved, (see chapter 5).

Although it was proposed by Charlie Taylor in his 2012 Report, headteachers cannot initiate a prosecution themselves. They may have delegated powers to issue Penalty Notices (see below) but *only* by formal agreement with their LA. Schools are required to provide copies, each personally signed by the headteacher, of the child's attendance record during the relevant 'period of complaint'. This period can go back *no further* than six months from the date the 'information' is laid before the court; 8-10 weeks of evidence is usually ample. There is no need for unauthorised absence to continue for six months before prosecution is even considered as seems to happen in some cases. LAs are expected to demonstrate that decisions are made in a timetabled way that avoids case 'drift'. Half a term is a long time in the educational life of a child if they are missing large amounts of school and from which they might never recover. *If* (and it's a very important 'if'), this action is what is needed to protect their best interests, then it should be done in a timely and efficient way.

The headteacher, or a key member of staff, may also be asked to provide a written statement, known as a 'Section 9 statement', outlining the criteria on which the absences have been left unauthorised and any inappropriate explanations provided by the parent. The offence is not difficult to prove, provided the grounds for not authorising the absences are clear. It is particularly important that no changes are made to school's attendance register that might conflict with the version presented to the court. This could undermine the entire case. Most arguments in court are about mitigation, such as the parent saying they cannot influence the child's behaviour or claiming that they have been bullied, rather than about whether an offence has occurred. It is an 'absolute' offence and 'not guilty' verdicts will be extremely rare if the LA has prepared its evidence properly and the school has acted correctly.

There are various statutory defences in s.444 on which the parent may rely, though, if they appear to have any merit, the LA should be unlikely to proceed in the first place. Here too, there are major implications for the school's record-keeping. Crucially, no offence is committed if the child is absent 'with leave' granted by someone at the school authorised to grant it, or if the parent can prove that the child should have been authorised to be absent due to sickness or some other 'unavoidable cause'. Authorisation means the school has agreed to the absence; parents cannot then be criticised for it. Failure to provide transport where the LA is required to do so and certain other statutory defences, such as religious festivals and a travelling lifestyle may also be cited.

Decisions taken by schools and LAs must at all times be 'reasonable'. As we will see later, this is a major issue with the growing use of Penalty Notices. If the parent chooses not to pay, which is their right, the LA is supposed to prosecute under s.444 instead, *based on the same evidence.* (They are not prosecuted for the non-payment, but for the original absence). Given that a Penalty Notice might now be issued for just a few days unauthorised absence, such as an unapproved holiday in term-time, it would be most unwise for LA procedures to allow them to be issued unless a significant total threshold has *also* been reached as a result. Otherwise the amount of evidence would almost certainly be seen by lawyers, councillors, or even by magistrates as too trivial and the whole process is then undermined. In general, prosecution should be used only for more substantial amounts of unauthorised absence, but if an LA uses Penalty Notices as well, it has to decide what to do if the parent does not pay. Many are just withdrawn which suggests to me at least that they should not have been issued in the first place. This seems to lead to a wide variety of practice, some of which, I would, argue, results in unjust and unreasonable proceedings against some parents.

Does prosecution work?

There is very little national evidence to go on. The National Foundation for Educational Research (NFER) published two reports in 2004 that concluded that prosecution was effective in about two-fifths of cases, in that the children concerned subsequently improved their attendance. ('School Attendance and the Prosecution of Parents: Effects and Effectiveness': NFER, 2004). But many LA officers and parents also reported that the proceedings often made little difference, or that the threat of court action was more use than actually going ahead with it, especially in response to situations that had already become entrenched. Further research by Ming Zhang at Cambridge University in 2007 came to very similar conclusions, (unpublished conference papers). Nothing always 'works' and in all situations.

There is a general signal from the government that 'good' LAs and schools are frequent users of the courts, though some would argue that having to prosecute a parent is a sign of failure that is always best avoided if possible. There is no obvious evidence that those LAs and schools that make most use of prosecution also have the best attendance figures; that would in any case be an unfair measure. Neither are prosecutions best evaluated by how high the fines are – some of which will not actually be paid or will be reduced later on appeal. Prosecution is time-consuming for the individual LA officer and little evidence is currently available that can demonstrate the facts one way or the other.

The 'enhanced offence' s.444(1A)

There is also the capacity for parents to be summonsed for the more serious offence under s. 444(1A) of 'parentally condoned unauthorised absence'. In effect all parental prosecutions should meet this criteria, and, in the light of the provisions of the Anti-social Behaviour Act 2003 (in England only – see below) some LAs may now use these more serious proceedings more regularly for cases that have not been resolved by other interventions, at least to begin with. Convictions at this level carry a maximum fine of £2,500 and up to three months in prison, so a parent can be forced to attend Court if they do not turn up for the hearing, (which cannot be required under s.444(1)). Such extreme sentences are rare. Even where they have been used, there have already been examples of parents who have previously served a prison sentence being prosecuted again for a further offence or immediate appeals replacing the original sentence with other less serious outcomes. Evidence is mixed. Prison is not necessarily a deterrent and solutions to family problems are rarely that simple. There will be many cases in which the view is taken that, despite the high level of absence, prosecution, fines and even imprisonment are not, in themselves, likely to improve the child's attendance or be what is best for them. Such an approach may be used more as an example to others than to bring about change in the family concerned, but action still has to be both fair and proportionate.

Anti-social Behaviour Act 2003 and Education (Penalty Notices) (England) Regulations 2004 (plus subsequent amendments)

New powers came into force from 2004, (in England only, though similar provision is now being discussed in Wales), that have given LAs the option of formalising their responses to non-attendance but without the need for parents to make a Court appearance. A Penalty Notice, along similar lines to a speeding fine, enables a parent to discharge their liability for unauthorised absences by paying a Penalty by post. Penalties are currently £60 (for each parent and each child concerned) if paid within 21 days or £120 if paid within 28 days. Payment must be made in full, not by instalments. A written warning must be issued first so they are normally still used as part of a casework procedure where the parent is deemed primarily responsible for the absence and has failed to respond to previous offers of help, attend meetings etc.

There has been pressure from the DfE for Penalty Notices to be issued for very small amounts of unauthorised absence and many LAs do so. But this raises many questions about reasonableness.

As indicated above, an LA is supposed to prosecute under s.444 if the parent chooses not to pay, as is their right; so that effectively means there must be as much evidence for a Penalty Notice as for any other case. Putting a parent before a Court because they haven't paid, when their child's overall attendance is 96% and they only have 10 unauthorised sessions in total, strikes me as wholly impractical as well as fundamentally unjust. Many other parents will commit far more offences but face no action. Some parents will see the fine as well worth paying anyway and, for example, simply add it to the cost of the holiday. (I have even heard that some travel agents will pay it for them!) But are these children and parents really a problem? In practice, some LAs seem to lose their nerve if they do not do pay and take no further action, so both the Warning and the Notice itself are effectively a bluff. That risks bringing the whole process into disrepute, even when it is appropriate.

In order to use Penalty Notices at all, an LA must draw up a Code of Conduct and agree it with their local schools and the Police. This will usually define a minimum number of relevant absences or an overall percentage of attendance as pre-conditions, but given these parameters, not all schools will choose to engage with the process in the same way. Some may wish to have the power devolved to them to issue the Notices on the LA's behalf. If so, it must be clear that they are still the LA's Notices and they can *only* be issued by a school in accordance with the agreed criteria, not unilaterally. But if you happen enrol your child in one of these schools, you may be far more likely to be fined than a parent behaving in exactly the same way, (perhaps even the same parent), whose child attends a school round the corner and whose practice is different.

In order to recognise this, any school where a Notice might be served must make parents aware of it in their attendance policy and be explicit about the 'threshold' that applies. I wonder how many do so. There could potentially be hundreds of Notices across an LA, and the numbers do vary enormously. Most LAs try to steer a middle path and may even have 2 sets of criteria which are applied differently, but again I have to ask what is the *purpose* of such a response? If the child is already a good attender, this is just a retrospective fine-collecting procedure which their educational or welfare needs do not require. It may be done solely to discourage others who may be more likely to keep to the school's expectation in future. But other children's circumstances might be very different. It is not as if holidays, for example, have been banned altogether – 'zero tolerance' is going beyond the wording of new regulation which confines 'leave' to 'exceptional circumstances' only; it does not remove the possibility completely. At its worst this whole process can look somewhat arbitrary and does nothing to meet the needs of those who are genuinely disaffected. This, more than anything, can look like ticking a box, not necessarily doing anything particularly useful.

Penalty Notices do have some potential as both a general deterrent and as a way of demonstrating a swift response to some parentally-condoned absence in order to prevent fairly low-level behaviours becoming more entrenched. I accept that and, where this is true and it helps the child or parent to re-engage more quickly, I can see the point. But if the child is already a chronic non-attender, it will almost certainly not be in their best interests for this procedure to be followed as it may simply delay making a more appropriate response while we have to wait a further 4 weeks to see if the parent will choose to pay. Experience suggests that some parents, perhaps especially those previously accustomed to attending courts, may choose not to pay the Penalty Notice and wait for their day in court (if it actually comes). They may then be able to negotiate some other penalty or payment of a potentially higher fine at a relatively small amount per week. That said, fining parents, in itself, does not of course ensure that the child or young person actually returns to school, which is all that really matters.

CHILDREN ACT 1989

Education Supervision Orders (see also chapter 5)

The Children Act 1989 is the framework for dealing with children who are experiencing family problems, both 'private law' (divorce etc.) and 'public law' (care proceedings, child protection etc.) The Act, implemented in October 1991, removed the power of the (then) LEA to apply to have a child taken into care for not attending school. Under previous legislation, certain grounds were listed which proved that the child's needs required the acquisition of parental rights by the LA. Absence from school was specifically included and for some children this led to alternative residential education on a far larger scale than would be considered appropriate (or affordable) today. However many of the children remained at home, sometimes still not attending school even if they were under a Care Order, and the cases were often given low priority by social workers whose authority and influence proved to be no greater than that of the parents.

Children Act 1989: SUMMARY

Education Supervision Order (s.36)

Places a child under the supervision of the LA on the grounds that he or she is not being 'properly educated'. The Order gives the 'supervisor' power to issue reasonable 'directions' to the child or parent about how the child should be educated. It is an offence by the parent if a direction given to them is not complied with.

General provisions for the welfare of children (s.17) and the 'welfare checklist' (s.1)

Family Proceedings Courts should pay attention to a child's 'educational needs' when making any decision about their lives in order to ensure that education is not adversely affected by the making of any Order. Education services are part of a network of local support for families to assist 'children in need'.

In practice, these powers were normally used only where there were other contributory risk factors as well, so the concept of 'significant harm' arising from the Act has not generally been seen as justifying intervention by social workers on school attendance grounds alone.

Older children who are refusing to go to school may well be 'beyond parental control', but whether the making of a Care Order will be better for them than no Order at all, (a key Children Act concept), is often an open question as it was before. Courts will not make Orders if the case for them has not been proven. There has been a move towards working with families on a non-statutory basis that not all teachers appreciate. There is, however, some frustration that this may leave some damaged children free to opt out of education entirely if they refuse to co-operate.

Under s.36, 'not being properly educated' is sufficient grounds for an ESO. This can be either because the child is a poor attender, (the issue of authorised/unauthorised is not important in this context as the education is still being missed and no offence is involved), or because there is evidence that nothing is being provided for a child supposedly being educated 'otherwise'. An ESO is supposed to be considered before *every* prosecution, but this rarely happens beyond a paper exercise, if at all. There is also a requirement to try to resolve problems by voluntary means first wherever possible and this has tended to mean that ESOs were sought only as a last resort when all else has failed, but when there is not much hope left of improvement. As I argue more fully in chapter 5, they are probably better used rather earlier, after a reasonable attempt at voluntary resolution, and work only in situations where the introduction of some external authority may help to promote more effective parenting. There always needs to be some dispute with the parent to justify any Order under the Children Act; the guidance says that only outright 'hostility' might make them unworkable. The supervisor can 'advise, assist and befriend' the child and give 'directions' to both the parents and the child in order to ensure the child is educated, including, for example, directing their admission to a new school if necessary.

These Orders are not made in the Magistrates Court but in the Family Proceedings Court where issues of care, child protection, residence after divorce etc. are also dealt with. They can be applied for only by LA officers. As with prosecutions, headteachers are again required to provide records of the child's attendance and a report outlining their educational needs and progress. There has to be a realistic expectation that the structure of the Order is likely to help the situation to improve, so it is vital that there is a clear sense of what the professionals wish to achieve but cannot currently do so because the LA has no authority to direct anyone. There has to be an Action Plan, to which the full commitment of the school is essential. The officers managing the Order will not provide the education themselves, so there has to be full consultation to ensure that it has a chance of success. Orders normally last for one year, but may be extended in exceptional circumstances. To me, this approach offers a potentially more constructive way forward that prosecution often will not. But many LAs have largely ignored these powers, either through lack of clear policy and resources, or because it is not entirely clear when they are best used. Allocating a supervisor to just one child is a major use of an LA officer's time and many will feel that they are better employed in working less intensively with a larger number of children. Government ministers have also been somewhat ambiguous about their value, (though they are still mentioned in the 2013 'Advice'), preferring to concentrate on more punitive approaches. I will come back later to how they might yet offer something useful.

General provisions for the welfare of children

The wider provisions of the Children Act are also relevant to education including where a child is considered at risk of 'significant harm' to their 'health or development' or in dealing with the consequences of abuse and other family problems. Although absence from school alone may not be sufficient grounds for statutory intervention, (and is not included in the definition of 'neglect'), action by social workers on wider grounds could take into account the failure by a parent to ensure their child goes to school, alongside other issues. It can certainly be a source of potential harm if a parent fails to ensure a child is educated, perhaps especially where they have SEN or a disability. Poor attendance, or the provision of no education 'otherwise' at all, should certainly be seen as a 'trigger' to merit investigation on the basis of promoting the child's best interests, not be dismissed as solely an 'educational' issue. That in no way reflects current thinking about 'joined-up' solutions to children's needs or the inspection requirements placed on LAs.

However, the test of 'significant harm' to a child's 'intellectual and social development' is a considerable one, though it might be relevant where parents are also neglecting the child in other ways. Social workers are not always aware of how important education is to a child's wellbeing. It is essential that school staff make a full contribution to any assessment being carried out into the child's needs. This process of joint working to support children and promote their best interests should operate under an agreed multi-dimensional Common Assessment Framework (or its local equivalent) that involves all agencies working with the child and family (see chapter 5). Teachers and other educational staff should expect to take the lead in carrying out such assessments where issues have arisen at school, including involving other agencies once the assessment has indicated what role they could play. Referring the child to someone else for them to do the assessment should now be less common and should only be necessary where action by another agency is clearly indicated or where concerns plainly relate to child protection. As the professional who already knows the child and family best, a teacher or non-teaching colleague may even be the 'lead professional', co-ordinating the work of others from outside the school, even if such a role will require a significant level of local training to support it.

School staff may also be asked to provide information about a child's educational career in the context of disputes about, for example, where the child should live following divorce, or a dispute between parents over the exercise of their 'parental responsibility'. This can be a difficult area in which staff will naturally be unwilling to be seen to be taking sides, but the Court may want to know, for example, any information that the school has about past involvement by the parents and their general attitude to education. Any information about a parent who had previously failed to ensure the child attended school, for example, would certainly be relevant. The Court is supposed to take education into account in *any* decision that may affect the child's welfare. As is also true for children in the 'looked-after' system, teachers should not be left to pick up the pieces of, for example, a move to a new carer, without the educational consequences of that decision being anticipated. Where will the child then go to school? How will they get there? Is a school place actually available?

This prior consideration does not always happen however, and parents always have the power to act unilaterally, unless there are Orders in force that specify the arrangements. School staff should see themselves as key agents in protecting the educational welfare of children, along with colleagues from the LA, and should therefore co-operate with any request for information or inter-agency plan. The new approach to SEND provision should make this process even more routine in future, notwithstanding the very real difficulties caused by pressure on resources and a frequent insufficiency of provision. But this holistic approach is not an optional extra; children, and their parents, are legally entitled to it.

REGISTRATION REGULATIONS
Education (Pupils` Attendance Records) Regulations 1991
These regulations created the 'performance tables' by requiring schools to report each year on their absence figures up to the end of May – but only for all children in National Curriculum Years 1-11 – now both authorised and unauthorised absences and up to the end of July (except for Year 11). These regulations also first permitted the use of computerised registration. Chapter 3 will look at daily registration in greater detail, but it is important to recognise that these requirements define very significant areas of legal practice concerning the admission and attendance of pupils of compulsory school age.

> *Registration Regulations: SUMMARY*
>
> **Education (Pupils' Attendance Records) Regulations 1991**
>
> *Created the concept of 'authorised' and 'unauthorised' absence and require every absence to be classified by the school as one or the other; allowed schools to use computerised registration systems.*
>
> **Education (Pupil Registration) (Amendment) Regulations 1997**
>
> *Allowed afternoon registration at any time in the session; introduced the fourth registration category of approved educational activity' for trips, work experience, college etc. (counts as present statistically).*
>
> **Education (Pupil Registration) (England) Regulations 2006**
>
> *Require the keeping of registers; define the circumstances under which children of compulsory school age may be removed from the Admission and Attendance registers; provision for leave of absence; inspection of registers by LA officers; preservation of registers etc.*
>
> *Amendments were made in 2010 allowing greater flexibility in schools' use of the Y code when children are unable to attend due to local or national disruption to transport, bad weather etc. More amendments came into force in September 2013 removing all reference to 'holidays' and '10 days' and making all leave at the discretion of the headteacher in 'exceptional' circumstances.*

Since 1991, schools have therefore been required to have appropriate systems for identifying which absences are unauthorised. As outlined previously, this decision determines whether or not the parent is committing an offence and so should obviously be made according to clear criteria. Some schools still authorise too generously or may never have established clear policies and procedures that are consistently applied by all staff. It should be clear whose responsibility it is to make a decision: the data manager; the class teacher; the year head, the headteacher? What procedures are in place for clarifying any uncertainties or challenging parents' explanations for absence?

The introduction of these regulations at first came to be associated with achieving as low as possible a figure for unauthorised absence, rather than defining clear expectations with parents as was the intention. Ultimately, the data provided for the published tables is not as important as ensuring that parents and children receive the right message about the importance of attendance. Low unauthorised absence does not necessarily mean high attendance; some schools authorise as many as 8-10% of sessions as legitimate absence, while others authorise less than 4%. This may suggest that different expectations are being applied, though the varying circumstances of schools also mean that there will inevitably be a wide diversity in the reasons for children's absences. This is the problem in using only the unauthorised figure as the measure of the 'problem'. Schools addressing their attendance responsibilities and being more strict with parents may see it rise, at least in the short term, which is hardly an incentive. But it should now be clear that *attendance* rather than only certain kinds of absence is the focus. This enables much fairer comparisons to be made between schools rather than comparing only absences that each school considers to be unauthorised, according to whatever criteria they each use.

The keeping of attendance records by computer has proved to be an extremely useful tool and several different systems are available, including those that monitor attendance at every lesson not just for each session. But it is important that the use of technology is not seen, as a solution to issues of poor attendance. More and more data, in itself, resolves nothing. As will explored in Chapter 4, it is the interpretation and use of the data that really matters, even allowing for the helpfulness of being able to do the calculations much more easily and the ease of producing an individual pupil's record. It may be extremely helpful, for example, to make a child's attendance history known to their parents on a regular basis and computerised printouts are ideal for this purpose.

Education (Pupil Registration) (Amendment) Regulations 1997

Historically, registers have always had to be marked at the beginning of each half-day session, (there must still be two sessions each day, however the timetable is structured). This is still the requirement for the morning, but from January 1st 1998 the (then) DFES gave schools some flexibility about when they can mark afternoon registers. This was intended to catch those pupils who go missing during the afternoon, but because registers are actually about parents, not children, it also raises a number of problems and few schools have seen the need for change. If attendance registers are not marked immediately after lunch, it is impossible for the staff to know during the afternoon session whether or not a given child is in school, without having to check individually. It is also impossible for a child to be late, providing they are there at the end, thus rendering all the rules about lateness irrelevant. In terms of safeguarding, a child could go missing for almost six hours and their absence not be officially noted. As the DFES advised at the time, schools choosing later registration arrangements for the afternoon would have to have other systems in addition for fire regulation purposes and for checking that children have not left at lunchtime. Many do, but these arrangements are not a substitute for the twice-daily mark. There are also some doubts about whether absence at the end of the session will be proof of an offence if a parent claims they were there at the beginning. To my knowledge this has yet to be tested in the Courts. All of this suggests that there is no value in making this change and that it will only cause other difficulties. The same expectations should apply in every school; there is no need for any variation about what is a universal duty that should treat every parent/child in the same way.

More importantly, these regulations also introduced a fourth registration category alongside present, authorised absent and unauthorised absent. Many schools would already have been counting those who are away from the premises for a legitimate reason such as an educational visit as 'present' for statistical purposes, (though the guidance actually says that children marked in this way are technically neither present nor absent – just 'counted as present'!) The previous regulations classed all those not on the premises as 'absent', even if the child was where they were supposed to be. This was plainly unreasonable. The revised regulation introduced the concept of an 'approved educational activity'. This covers:

- approved work experience for older pupils;
- field trips and educational visits;
- approved sporting activities and interviews;
- link courses/FE Colleges and other alternative provision;
- 'guest' pupils receiving part of their education at another school or unit while remaining the responsibility of the school where registered.

This change is *not* intended to cover children who have been given leave of absence to 'work at home' while remaining a registered pupil, such as those with a long-term illness, on a part-time timetable and those on study leave or 'flexi-schooled'. They still have to be classed as authorised absent as the amount of education they will be receiving is not considered sufficient or under the close supervision of a teacher. This also applies to children in hospital where their status as ill is seen as dominant; they too still have to be classed as authorised absent unless they are known to have done some supervised work with a suitable teacher for at least part of that session. Where education is taking place away from the school building itself, it is, of course, essential for schools to have systems in place that check the pupil actually attended as required. The coding system cannot be a blanket arrangement to class as present sessions in which the pupil did not comply with an agreed arrangement – these would still be *unauthorised* absences.

Education (Pupil Registration) (England) Regulations 2006 and later amendments

Maintaining an admission register (Regs.4,5.6)

The admission register will now routinely be kept by means of a computerised system. It must include known information about parents as well as the children (including those with parental responsibility living apart from their child wherever possible). Data collection systems must be set up in a way that asks the right questions on admission and updates the information annually. This should include the school the child last attended, if any, and the admission date. Schools should also record which LA the pupil lives in if it is different from the authority where the school is. This will be essential information for enabling any inter-agency involvement later. A child cannot be on the admission register but not on the attendance register (or vice versa) and there is no such thing as a 'trial' admission in which the pupil attends but is not marked in the registers for a period of time. The only exception should be where they have still been retained on an admission and attendance register elsewhere for the time being under a 'managed move' or are just visiting for odd lessons as a 'guest'. If not currently registered elsewhere, a child must be considered a 'registered pupil' from the first day that they were *expected* at the school and an attendance record must be kept from that date. This is essential to avoid children being left between, for example, two schools, neither of which accepts that he/she is their pupil or is recording them as absent.

Leave in term-time (Reg. 7)

Regulation 7 has been amended from September 2013 to make it clear that all leave is at the headteacher's discretion in 'exceptional circumstances' only. There never was any automatic entitlement; only discretion to grant leave 'up to ten days' per school year to 'go away on holiday' if appropriate. Both these terms have now been removed. The concept of 'extended leave' has also been removed; it all requires the consent of the headteacher on an individual basis. Schools should develop clear policies and procedures on this issue.

Deletions from the admission register (Reg. 8)

This is perhaps the most important regulation of them all if it is children's welfare that is the primary concern. Neither schools nor parents are free remove children of compulsory school age from the registers as they wish. Doing so means they are no longer a 'registered pupil' and changes the child's legal status to 'educated otherwise' *de facto*. It therefore removes entirely the legal obligation on the parent to ensure they attend and leaves the child without educational provision unless the action is within the regulations. Children cannot be removed from the attendance register but remain on an informal or 'shadow' roll. Even those on long term home tuition or other alternative programmes, if they are still registered pupils who are included within the school's Census returns (and for whom the school is therefore still being funded), must receive a mark for *every* session. The most common situations in which children's names *may* be legally deleted are:

- *when the child 'has been registered' at another school/unit.* Children should not therefore be removed from the registers on a 'promise' by parents, only when the school is informed *by another school* that they have actually admitted the child (or after four weeks if they have moved away from their last known address but no subsequent school has been in contact – see below).

- *when the parent has given written notification to the school that they are educating the child 'otherwise' than at school.* The school must then inform the LA's home education monitoring officer.

- *when the child has stopped attending and is no longer 'ordinarily resides' at a place which is a reasonable distance from the current school.* This does *not* give the school power to remove the name of a child either because they have stopped attending but are still living at the same address, or just because the family have moved a short distance. It only covers children who have physically moved away *and* stopped coming, after four weeks. Parents may wish to continue transporting the child even from some distance away. If so, they still have a right to a place; it is not automatically lost because they have moved. If the child no longer attends and there is no contact from any other school, the LA *must* be informed so that checks can be made about whether the child has been admitted elsewhere. The pupil should remain on the registers during this period as 'unauthorised absent' until their position is clear. Pupils should not be removed from the admission register because they have committed an offence or gone into some form of custody, unless the sentence is over four months. If the expectation is that they will be returning home after a few weeks, as is usually the case, they will be entitled to return to the school unless the offence was within the head's jurisdiction and also merited permanent exclusion. (They can be marked as present at an 'approved educational activity' while in custody without, in this case, their school having to check each day!)

- *when the child has not returned within ten more school days after exceptional leave of absence, except by virtue of illness or other unavoidable cause known to the school.* These children may reasonably be assumed not to be coming back so the school does not have to carry the absences indefinitely. (Unless there are safeguarding concerns, it may be reasonable to remove children from the registers if it is known that they have gone abroad for an extended period or if the trip is open-ended. The child could then be re-admitted if they return).

- *after four weeks continuous unauthorised absence and 'both the proprietor of the school and the local education authority have failed, after reasonable enquiry, to locate the pupil.'* This is for use *only* where the pupil has disappeared/moved to an *unknown* address, not for situations where he/she is refusing to attend but still resident in the same place. The school cannot act without consultation with the LA first to make a joint decision. Schools must ensure that information about any missing pupil removed from their registers is recorded onto the Lost Pupils database (via School2School) as an alternative to the usual Common Transfer File (CTF) arrangements. This is a vital safeguard.

- *at the end of the process of any permanent exclusion* i.e. not until all necessary representations have been made, to the governors and, if applicable, to the Independent Panel, not from the day of the exclusion itself. Schools and LAs must still provide work for the child to do during this process, and on a full-time basis from the sixth day. If the pupil actually attends some alternative provision, an exclusions centre for example, while still excluded, this should be classed as present. The 2013 *'Advice'* and the DfE guidance on exclusions both repeat the statement that removing the child from the admission register without due process as a form of 'unofficial exclusion' is illegal.

Other situations cover where the pupil has died, or is judged permanently medically unfit for school until they will be old enough to leave or where they cease to be of compulsory school age. Deletions outside these rules usually cause on-going problems for everyone.

All of this detail is intended to ensure that there are no children whose status is unclear or who are 'lost' to the system. This is how children end up not receiving any education for years on end, with all the consequences for them and for the wider community. Where children are not in school, it must be clear which are registered pupils but absent, and which are being educated in some other way. There should be no other alternatives.

Inspection of registers/making copies (Regs. 10, 11, 12)

Maintained schools must make their registers available for inspection by authorised LA officers. *All* schools must do so for Ofsted and other inspectors. LA officers must also be permitted to make copies for courts etc.

Within this extensive variety of legal sources it is possible to discern certain principles which, while not always entirely consistent with one another, need to be held alongside each other to ensure good practice in dealing with attendance and absence issues:

Promoting participation

The government believes that all children should have the opportunity to benefit from education. School attendance is not optional for parents once their children become registered pupils; it is a key part of their parental duty and a legal entitlement for their children. Schools are accountable for the levels of attendance of their pupils in order to ensure that the right of every child to receive an education is not overlooked. The right to receive an education does not have to be earned.

Working in partnership

While the LA has the final statutory responsibility for ensuring that the duty on parents is carried out, these joint responsibilities are best approached by partnership between all those involved. This includes the school, the parents, the child, the LA and any other relevant agencies with an interest in the welfare of children. No-one should act unilaterally.

Using statutory powers appropriately

When problems arise, an approach based on securing the co-operation of parents through negotiated agreements should be attempted wherever possible. However, enforcement or other legal procedures should be used in situations where the welfare of the child is at risk, where parents have persistently failed to act responsibly and in order to protect their children's best interests.

CHAPTER 3

EFFECTIVE REGISTRATION

GENERAL

This chapter should be read in conjunction with the various regulations (see chapter 2) and the current '*Advice on School Attendance*', issued by the DfE in November 2013. Registration is often seen as an unwelcome chore by both staff and children. But marking registers properly is fundamental to a whole-school approach to promoting attendance and a vital element of evidence-gathering in the event of parental prosecution. It is also an essential part of the school's pastoral system. This is where pupils and parents are most likely to notice whether absence actually matters to anyone and where staff should be identifying those who need an individual response. Registration should be a significant expression of the school's duty of care for the pupils and is a useful time for the sharing of information, the identification of problems and the reinforcement of the need to bring in parental notes after an absence etc. The arrangements should therefore be a key part of a school's written attendance policy, alongside targets, reward strategies and incentive schemes, appropriate responses to unauthorised absence and effective working relationships with parents and other professionals, (see later chapters).

There is an argument that it has all become too easy for everybody, parents, staff and pupils, now that computers do most of the work. Indeed, registration may now consist only of the few seconds it takes to identify those who are not there before getting on with the 'real' business of the lesson. This is a mistake. It should feel like something has been missed if you are not there; otherwise, why bother coming? The current Ofsted Framework places almost as much emphasis on punctuality as it does on attendance and in my opinion there is still a strong case for a proper, if brief, 'registration period' at the beginning of each session in which a member of staff can both identify the missing and reward those who are present. If the school uses every lesson registration as well, it must be clear which marks record whether or not the parent has fulfilled their duty in presenting the child on time for that *whole session*. (Every lesson checks do not need to be as prominent as formal session registration. Although they are important for other reasons, including safeguarding, they do not carry the same legal significance). The quality of practice at this point is often an indicator of a school`s general awareness of wider welfare issues.

Registration categories

There are five registration categories, no matter how many codes are used to indicate different circumstances. For every session, all pupils of compulsory school age who are included on the admission register, including those who may be receiving their education elsewhere, must be marked as either:

- *present (at the school);*

- *authorised absent (with the school's permission)*

- *unauthorised absent (without the school's permission)*

- *attending an 'approved educational activity' (not actually at the school but engaged in supervised education and therefore 'counted as present'), or*

- *unable to attend due to temporary school closure; failure of official transport; widespread travel disruption due to snow etc. (These sessions are not counted as absences or attendances).*

It is essential to be consistent throughout the school in the definitions used, especially of authorised and unauthorised absence. The DfE guidance, together with any procedures provided by the

LA, should be followed by all staff, not just those who choose to do so! Parents and children should not be faced with differing expectations according to who is marking the register or, if possible, across neighbouring schools that their children attend. There must be, in particular, a *standard system* for recording absences, especially the codes entered in the registers to indicate on what grounds absences have been authorised. A provisional mark can be entered, to be clarified later in the light of further information, though this should not result in the wholesale authorisation of absences many months later, simply on the parent's signature.

The 2013 DfE *'Advice'* contains a set of recommended codes. These are not actually mandatory but if a school uses any different system it must still contain the same information. Schools cannot change the 'statistical meaning' of the various codes as these are now incorporated into the School Census which simply reads the data the school has entered. (No forms are now involved so whatever you put in will be whatever you get out. It is wise to make sure the data is properly audited before it is sent). This whole process certainly enables much more effective analysis of the reasons for absence in individual schools than used to be available, but whether it provides a fair basis for comparison between them is a moot point. There is still plenty of room for interpretation and some of the issues raised here in summary are explored in more detail later in the chapter. Note that these codes relate *only* to pupils of compulsory school age. Outside those parameters there can be no unauthorised absence, just absence with or without the school's permission, or sessions that are discounted.

REGISTRATION CODES

/ present (a.m.) and \ present (p.m.)

Surely there's no room for confusion here? I'm afraid there's plenty. Remember, registration is essentially about the *parent's* legal duty to make sure their child is educated, not about monitoring the behaviour of the child. So the legal requirement is that the child is physically present when the register is called; that may not necessarily mean they were there for the whole session. Once the correct mark has been entered it cannot be changed, even if the child later goes home ill or leaves the premises without permission. This is the irony about true 'truancy'; if you get your mark and then walk out, the published data will still record you as 'present'. Morning registration must be taken at the beginning of the day; afternoon registration is best done at the beginning too in my view, though this is not a legal requirement as long as it is still done. But how late can you arrive and still get a mark? That's entirely at the school's discretion though caselaw has established that allowing up to 30 minutes is reasonable. After that, you can be marked unauthorised absent even if you come. Some schools (or even different individuals within a school) might mark you absent after 5 minutes; others will keep their registers open all morning and count you as present whenever you arrive. It's not the recommended practice but it's not illegal. Some late arrivals are legitimate and unavoidable; those children might end up with presents or absences depending on their school's interpretation. So many of those marked as present might not actually have been there for the whole session – we just don't know.

B: attending alternative provision away from the school site (counts as present)

This mark is a major factor in uncertainty about the validity of the figures and raises very significant questions about children's welfare unless it is used responsibly. Increasing numbers of pupils, especially those with behavioural difficulties and at KS4 do not necessarily receive all their education in their own school building. Quite rightly it enables an attendance to be recorded when the pupil is where they are supposed to be; college, special unit, alternative provision etc. (It may also be used for young people on supervised internet-based distance learning programmes, some of whom may never physically attend the school at all). The problem is, schools often don't check whether the pupil is actually there today. Indeed I have seen plenty of examples of B codes entered in advance which is obviously unacceptable. It is extremely tempting to record an attendance anyway, especially as many of the children engaged in more flexible programmes might not have been the best attenders in the past. But it is very poor practice and may raise important safeguarding concerns if the registers suggest that the pupil is engaging in supervised education for that session but in fact they are not. In my experience, this is extremely common and, of course, it artificially inflates both the pupil's and the school's attendance. I have known an Ofsted inspector, noting that the number of pupils actually in the school from a particular year group was significantly fewer than the recorded level of attendance, to ask exactly where all the others were – and she expected an answer in each individual case by mid-morning break. B is also sometimes incorrectly used for pupils allowed to 'work at home' under their parent's supervision. But these children are not in fact receiving the full-time education to which they are entitled. The DfE *'Advice'* clearly states that any such sessions are authorised absences, *not* to be counted as present. But if a school uses the B code who would know? It may seem to solve everyone's problem and improve the data as well.

C: approved 'leave' in exceptional circumstances (authorised absent)

This is the code, designed to be used at the headteacher's discretion, for any session of absence agreed as 'leave' but which isn't covered by any of the other marks! It is meant for things like weddings, bereavements and unexpected family crises, just for a day or two. But it also has to be used for so-called 'flexi-schooling' which may go on indefinitely and for 'extended leave' which no longer has a mark of its own. Many schools will also use it for 'unofficial' exclusions, including children sent home while a meeting is arranged or a scarce resource is applied for, without any alternative provision being made available in the meantime which would be legally required if the exclusion had been done properly. This is not just an issue of correct practice; there is no power to send a child home indefinitely, to prevent them attending or to remove their place at the school without due process.

If the circumstances are truly exceptional, such as the child posing a serious risk to other children, a managed procedure should be put in place with the relevant LA to protect their welfare and ensure continuity of provision. Otherwise children can end up out of school for months or even years. This is one of the marks that may therefore *increase* the amount of absence, but all of it is authorised so it doesn't show up as 'truancy', even though the pupil may be out and about and get picked up on a patrol looking for those who are not attending. It is also often used for children who are taking part in legitimate licensed 'performances' in theatre, film. TV etc. in school-time as this doesn't have its own code. (That means we don't know how much of this kind of absence there is. Some children may have quite a lot of time away from school, as much as a family holiday for example, but without the same risk of censure).

D: pupils who are dual registered at two schools (discounted)

There are not very many of these but this is a significant and recent change. It only applies where children are registered at two schools (including PRUs), not to other kinds of alternative provision. Only the school where they are supposed to be has to record a present or absent mark for that session. The other school can discount it from their data. So if the pupil is currently expected to attend a PRU or special school full-time, for example, their 'home' school can enter a D for all the sessions. The PRU is responsible for recording their actual attendance and absence. This has been a help in situations where schools have previously felt they were being penalised for the pupil's absence elsewhere. It also acted as a disincentive for making such arrangements where the child needed them, which should no longer be the case.

E: excluded, fixed term and permanent until confirmed by the governors (authorised absent)

There should never be more than 5 days in a row of this mark because there is an obligation on schools and LAs to make alternative full-time provision for the pupil from the 6th day, even if the exclusion is continuing. From that point on they should receive a B (or an absent mark if they don't go) relating to whatever their alternative provision is. Inspectors (or even the DfE) may pick up long rows of Es, but a B mark might not reflect what is actually happening. Once a fixed period exclusion is over, the child must be allowed to return, even if parents have not attended a meeting or responded to letters etc. Exclusions cannot be open-ended. A whole series of separate 5 days can be used up to a maximum of 45 in a school year but if the exclusion is more than 5 days continuously there *must* be other full-time provision made, away from the school or in a shared unit.

F: agreed extended leave (authorised absent) No longer recommended.

This Code has disappeared from the DfE *'Advice'* with the change of the regulation from September 2013, but that doesn't mean that parents won't still request it! Clearly some longer trips abroad in particular are truly exceptional. Some children, especially those from some ethnic minorities, will still leave the country with their family for considerable periods of time to visit relatives etc. These are not just 'holidays'. Schools can deal with this situation in a variety of ways. This was the mark for those that are kept on the admission register and their leave was authorised; (now it would have to be C; see G below if it is not authorised). But, if the absence is for more than 4 weeks, or if parents have not been able to say exactly when they will be returning, many schools will interpret the regulations as allowing them to remove the child from their admission register and avoid the absences altogether as they have, in effect 'moved away'. The school may give a promise that a place will be made available again if they return, though some may then have difficulty getting back into the same school when they return if it is over-subscribed. Despite this complication I don't have a problem with that approach myself. It seems only fair on both the parent and the school – you shouldn't be classed as 'absent' if you're currently in India for several weeks or months. The problem is that so much depends on individual discretion and the school down the road may not do the same, despite the fact that this will increase their level of absence. Comparisons will then be made which suggest that one school has less overall or persistent absence than another, or even less 'truancy', but clearly that may not be the case if the schools have just used different strategies in response to the same situation.

G: holiday leave that has not been agreed by the school (unauthorised absent)

All references to 'holidays' or to '10 days' have also been removed from the regulations, but of course some families will still go. It is not possible to legislate against parents taking holidays, only against schools authorising them. So what will their schools do? This is one of only 3 codes that provide evidence of an offence but the numbers have traditionally been extremely small. They are likely to become more common in future, but it entirely depends on the school's response. A holiday may all be marked as G if it has a strict policy or if the leave wasn't approved in advance for this particular child; or some may be approved and some not approved, or it may all be approved. The behaviour, taking the holiday, is the same in every case, so what does the data actually tell us? The issue will also arise about what action can result from just a few isolated days unauthorised absence. Many LAs will take the view that this is not sufficient evidence for a prosecution so no legal action may be possible. A school may have delegated authority to issue a Penalty Notice in such circumstances, but the same question will arise if the parents choose not to pay it. If no action then results many might ask what was the point of marking it unauthorised in the first place, especially as this might also be used as a judgment against the school as 'truancy'?

H: approved holiday (authorised absent)

This code can still be used if the school considers the holiday request 'exceptional'. But what does 'exceptional' mean? It will all depend on the school's interpretation. Taking a holiday is clearly not a parental 'entitlement' as many have assumed, (it never was), but neither is it necessarily classed as an offence if you do it anyway. It might or might not be authorised and decisions by agencies have to be 'reasonable'. The data entered, and its significance, is therefore all down to how the individual school chooses to respond. I continue to maintain, as do some headteachers I know, especially those in areas of disadvantage, that a short holiday with your parents at the only time they can afford it, if avoiding certain crucial weeks, is not necessarily a bad thing for the child. I agree that better-off families should be discouraged from taking frequent breaks, but it may be unrealistic to expect them to be fined if their child is always in school the rest of the time. I am not sure that this change will be worth all the hassle in the long run and it has certainly reinforced some unhelpful stereotypes about 'irresponsible' parents and 'out-of-touch' schools.

I: illness (authorised absent)

This mark accounts for the overwhelming majority of absences, 3 or 4 times the total amount of unauthorised absence, and is therefore not a problem, at least in terms of alleged 'truancy'. If the school agrees the child was genuinely ill, parents have an immediate defence in law. Some children, especially those in poorer communities and those with special educational needs, get ill more often than others. This is clearly reflected in the data and I'm not sure schools in some areas and many special schools can often do much about it other than encouraging an early return if it is safe for the child to do so. But it certainly has a major impact on both overall and persistent absence which can seem rather unfair. (Both I and my daughter would have been 'persistent absentees' for this reason using current criteria!) If the school *doesn't* really accept that the child was ill, then they shouldn't authorise it. But many do for the obvious reason of reducing their unauthorised absence and because they may have no choice in practice but to take the parent's word for it. Notes from doctors cannot be required and are usually not available. (Even explanations from parents do not legally have to be in writing). LA officers may be able to help find out the truth if there is any dispute but ultimately the school has to decide what to do.

J: Attending an interview at another school or prospective employer (counts as present)

Only needed if the pupil misses the whole session, not if they come to school first, again, provided they actually went.

L: late before the registers are closed (present)

This is a big decision for a school because it makes the difference not just between whether or not an absence is authorised but between being counted as absent or present. (See below for a more thorough exploration of the issues). As was discussed above, there is no regulation about when this judgment should be made and practice therefore varies. What is too late in one school to get a mark (see U below) will be marked as L in another and therefore classed as present. That may make a big difference to the published information, though what actually happened may be identical. Exactly who makes the decision, and according to what criteria, is often unclear. Obviously there is pressure to be generous and therefore to avoid the absences.

M: medical or dental appointment (authorised absent)

This mark is only supposed to be used when the child is absent at registration and also misses the *whole* session for what is agreed by the school to be a legitimate medical or dental appointment. It is not meant to be used for illnesses as some schools still do, (partly because I looks very much like / or \ and is therefore much harder to spot in the computerised and printed records than M). Neither should it be used if the child only misses part of the session; schools may be recording absences unnecessarily in these cases.

N: no explanation yet received (unauthorised absent)

This is a temporary mark pending further enquiries and should not appear at all in the final records. But the regulations do not specify when such a decision must be made. Returns have to be made to the DfE termly and there should certainly be no Ns (or blanks) left by then. But that means it can be unclear for several weeks what the status of that particular session is. Many N marks are subsequently turned into authorised absences and some schools even send out lists of unresolved dates to parents for them to explain retrospectively all in one go. Other schools wouldn't do this so will end up with more unauthorised absences as a result. The overall attendance figures are the same either way, so it all depends on what's being counted.

O: no satisfactory explanation received (unauthorised absent)

This is the only mark (with G and U) that can prove an offence by the parent and entirely depends on the school choosing to enter it. Absences can be left unauthorised for a variety of reasons and it may happen just because the school's systems for registration, collecting notes and seeking explanations are less than efficient. O cannot be used for any session where the pupil was asked not to attend, (such as an unofficial exclusion), and the parent has a defence if they can demonstrate that the absence was in fact 'unavoidable' and should therefore have been authorised. So the criteria have to be clear, widely understood and equitable. This should not be a matter for individual judgment but be implemented consistently in line with the school's clearly-defined policies.

P: approved sporting activity (counts as present)

This mark is intended only for pupils missing a whole session because they are participating in a sporting event on behalf of the school, (not just for those watching). Registers can usually be marked before they go unless it is a tour. Some LAs may also recommend using this rather than C for approved 'performances' but that does then class the sessions as an attendance which is rather controversial.

R: religious festival (authorised absent)

This is one of the marks that affects some schools much more than others and undoubtedly can have a significant impact on their overall figures. Originally it was intended to cover only isolated Christian festivals that fall on a school day such as Ascension Day. But now Eid and Ramadan will account for nearly all of them if they fall in term-time. Schools with a high percentage of children from certain ethnic and religious communities will inevitably suffer an unavoidable impact on their overall data as a result. Headteachers have no choice but to enter this mark if the parent requests it as it is a specific defence, unless it is decided to close on days when attendance would otherwise be badly affected, as some schools with the freedom to vary how often they open are now able to do. It is unlikely that those days will be made up elsewhere so that might be seen by other schools with high levels of absence on those days as somewhat unfair.

S: study leave (authorised absent)

If the best educational outcomes for the children are the driving factor, this mark should now be very rare as children are not best prepared for examinations by staying in bed or watching Jeremy Kyle! They need to be in school revising and preparing for what comes next. If the school enters an S that will be classed as authorised absent. But some still using study leave will choose to enter a B, and therefore to record an attendance, even though B is only meant to be used for educational activities that are properly supervised not for 'working at home'. Importantly, DfE Advice is that schools must offer an alternative to study leave if they use it. Parents still have a duty and children still have a right to be at school. Many parents would prefer their child not to be at home at such a crucial time. I wonder how many schools make this clear? In future, Y11 data may well be collected to the end of June. Schools will then be expected to make provision right up to the leaving date, which is surely commensurate with the new 'expectation of participation' beyond Year 11? Neither should S (or any other code) be used for 'review days'. This is not an appropriate use of any school day – the DfE and I are in agreement here, at least until they change it again under pressure as they did with the prohibition of 'flexi-schooling'.

T: absence for a child from the travelling community (authorised absent)

A child may live in a family 'whose business requires them to travel from place to place' as the legislation still rather quaintly puts it. This mark is only meant to be used where the family is actually away travelling but I have also seen it used for a child from the traveller culture who is just absent at home, which is against the DfE *Advice*. As one of the most educationally marginalised groups of all, this mark is intended to make sure that children from the Gypsy, Roma and travelling community don't lose their school place while they're away. But of course it can mean large numbers of authorised absences about which nothing can be done but which count against the school for overall and persistent absence purposes. These children may even be in another school elsewhere or in some kind of provision, (which would enable the school to record a D or a B instead), but usually their home school doesn't know where they are. In practice, such children are likely to be off-registered if they disappear for more than four weeks. Not necessarily the best practice but entirely understandable. Schools should at least make every effort to keep in touch with the children while they are away if at all possible.

U: late after registration (unauthorised absent)

See below for a more extensive discussion of lateness, but as we have seen under L above this all depends on the school's decision about when the registers are closed. The more strict you are the more U marks you will end up with, and vice versa. These sessions *can* be used as the basis of a parental prosecution but that is very unlikely if there are no other unauthorised absences as well, so many schools won't see the point in using it and undermining their own performance as a result, unless prosecution on other grounds is actively being considered by the LA.

V: educational visit and W: work experience (count as present)

Perfectly reasonable – as long as the child or young person went, as with the B and J codes, not just as a blanket mark for a whole class irrespective of what the individual children actually did.

X: for use only with pupils not of compulsory school age (not counted)

Schools still have to enter something in their registers for sessions when those outside compulsory age are not there. The DfE is now collecting data on the Reception year, though it will not (currently) be published as part of the school's performance data and it may not be particularly useful as the criteria used will vary. Such attendance, by definition, is not compulsory and does not have to be full-time, so what does 'absence' tell us? Indeed, if this mark is used, there will be no absences. All these schools are doing, as with sixth forms, is keeping a record of when the child was in the building. The usual purpose of registration does not apply in this context. So /, \ and X are really all that is required to cover whether or not they are there. X must, however, never be used for a child who *is* of compulsory school age.

Y: enforced school closure (not counted)

This has also recently changed which is why comparison with previous years' data is misleading from 2011 onwards. Once the persistent absence measurement was introduced, which meant that all children then under 80% attendance, (now 85%), were identified as a potential problem, there was an outcry from headteachers and parents in times of bad weather, airport closures and other local transport difficulties. Many children could not get to school. So now headteachers can use their discretion to keep the school open but to discount any missed sessions where they consider it reasonable to do so in these kinds of circumstances. They don't therefore count as absences as they did before. It may also be interpreted as appropriate for times when schools close to some pupils because of phased year-group entry, boiler breakdowns, flu epidemics, staff shortages, industrial action etc., though this is not actually specified in the guidance. (Even though academies are free to vary it, does any maintained school actually open to *all* their pupils for 190 days a year as the law requires?) 'Leave' has to be distinguished from 'school closed' in these circumstances, but removing the session from the data is obviously more advantageous than recording authorised absences.

Z: Pupil not yet admitted (not counted)

This is only for temporary use where pupils in a pre-admission group were entered onto the registration system in advance, but never actually arrived. If a school is subsequently deleting these children from the registers, they must be reported to the LA if they are not known to have been admitted elsewhere instead.

School closed to pupils (not counted)

INSET days, occasional days. election days, as well as the period between terms etc. when the teachers may be working but the pupils are not. These days do not count towards the year total for the pupils.

The choice of the relevant code and deciding whether the absence is authorised is the school's responsibility, not the parent's. The attendance policy should make this clear. *Each* authorised absence must show the relevant code for that half-day session. The majority will be for sickness and other legitimate reasons, but the headteacher and governors should ensure that clear guidance is given to staff and that agreed procedures are actually followed. Senior staff should be constantly monitoring the practice of those with day-to-day responsibility and ensuring that any uncertainties are dealt with properly. At its worst, this power can lead to a school effectively colluding with parents in allowing children to be absent when they should have attended. Normally only *unavoidable* absences should ever be authorised unless the school agrees that leave is appropriate. This does not mean that any explanation that is offered by a parent has to be accepted as grounds for authorisation. A note, in itself, is not sufficient; it depends on what the note says.

If authorisation is used over-generously, this may send a signal to parents and children that attendance is not important and that obtaining authorisation is easy. The sole aim at all times is to encourage the child back to school as early as reasonably possible, *not* to find an explanation for the absence so that it can be authorised. Clear procedures should be in place, especially where staff feel that too many absences are being accounted for by parental notes. It is good practice to indicate to the parents that absences will not be authorised in future without some additional assurance that the absences were truly unavoidable. This may lead to an increase in unauthorised absence; it should also lead to an increase in attendance, (the primary objective) as parents and pupils come to see that the school will not simply grant permission without question.

THEMED STUDY 1

DEFINING 'UNAVOIDABLE' ABSENCE

An LA once prosecuted a parent for failing to ensure her 15 year-old daughter attended school. The defence argued that the cause of the child's absence was 'unavoidable' because she had a child of her own to look after. The parent's argument was accepted and the case was dismissed, though this decision was later overturned on appeal. It obviously wasn't clear what 'unavoidable' means.

Bringing this case to Court at all was a mistake. It is often not reasonable to expect children of compulsory school age who become mothers also to attend school, though this should not be assumed automatically and some schools make specific provision for childcare to support those in this situation. If not, there are usually alternatives which can adequately satisfy legal requirements if required. But the case raises the importance of the fact that absence due to an 'unavoidable cause' is not an offence (Education Act 1996 s.444(3)(b)). Parents do not necessarily commit an offence just because the child is absent and the question of definition will often determine

---

whether or not an LA has any power to take proceedings against them or issue Penalty Notice.

Take, for example, the persistent 'truant'; that is, the child who chooses either to absent themselves from school on a regular basis or who regularly fails to stay for the whole day. If they have already been marked present, that mark cannot be cancelled subsequently so there is no evidence that can be used against the parents. If they have missed the whole session, the absence may have been 'avoidable' in the sense that the child could have chosen otherwise, but a parent, (who is the only person who can commit the offence, not the pupil), might argue, especially in relation to an older child, that they had done everything reasonable to prevent the situation occurring.

They may have woken the child in time to go to school, provided the uniform and dinner money, rung the school to check they had arrived, even taken them to school themselves or responded immediately every time the school alerted them to the child going missing. All such strategies might fail and the child refuse to cooperate. If, despite the parent's best efforts, the child still fails to attend, such absence might be seen as 'unavoidable' as far as the parent is concerned. Courts, however, do not usually accept such an argument. The parent has to accept liability even if they feel powerless, but they may well receive a sympathetic hearing and only a minimal penalty that renders the whole process fairly pointless. Nothing in this procedure will necessarily change the child's behaviour, which is what really needs addressing.

This should cause school staff to reflect on the way in which they authorise pupils to be absent. In doing so, they are recognising that the 'unavoidable' criteria apply and that no offence occurs. There are basically only two grounds for authorising an absence:

(a) 'leave' granted by the school, i.e. situations where it is agreed, ideally in advance, that the child is not required to attend: exclusions, study leave, exceptional leave, medical appointments, religious festivals, children licensed to appear in an entertainment etc. These are largely defined by regulations where the school is required to grant leave if the appropriate criteria apply.

(b) explanations for absence provided by the parent that are accepted by the school as 'unavoidable': illness, family crises and emergencies etc. These are much more a matter of the parent taking the initiative in keeping the child away from school and the headteacher then having to decide whether or not to accept their explanation.

Both categories require every school to have a clear sense of what is acceptable, and to make this very clear to parents. In the case of the young mother, for example, many schools might have authorised the absences on the grounds that she could not reasonably be expected to attend. They may have sent work home, or agreed with parents that home tuition be provided. There could then have been no prosecution as there would have been no evidence, but neither would she have been still receiving a proper education.

Only absences that the school judges to be 'avoidable' are relevant to whether an offence is being committed by the parent. The LA may advise but it is not its decision. The evidence produced is an exact copy of the school register, marked in accordance with the school's attendance policy, and for which the headteacher is accountable in the event of any dispute. So it is vital that schools do not describe absences as 'unavoidable', and therefore authorise them, too readily. It is not simply the existence of an explanation provided by the parent that determines this decision; it is the nature of the explanation given. Even with quite significant health problems, a child might still be reasonably expected to attend. Children with temporary injuries or with minor fractures can often still be accommodated. The intention of the legislation is that there must be no reasonable way in which the child could have managed to come to school before the absence should be authorised.

This means that a whole range of possible reasons for absence should not be accepted automatically; it depends on the circumstances. Staying at home to look after younger siblings would not normally be unavoidable, but it might be if the child is also a carer for a parent with a disability or in an emergency. Shopping rarely has to be done in school time. Daytrips might reasonably wait for weekends and holidays, but there might be extenuating circumstances when, perhaps, relatives are visiting from abroad or the child has won a prize. Some absences may be reasonable, especially if the child is normally a good attender, even if they are not strictly 'unavoidable', (if, for example, this is the only time the parent can take a family holiday).

But the published absence figures still suggest that some schools are authorising too generously, even allowing for flu epidemics and other local circumstances, though a few individuals might reasonably reach a high level and some special schools might simply be responding to exceptional circumstances. Written school attendance policies should make it clear that the school will not accept any explanation as grounds for authorisation, though it must do so if the absence is reasonable. Any dispute about this in court will have to be referred to the headteacher who would then have to appear in person to explain the basis of the decisions. As few people as possible should be involved where there is any uncertainty. Experience suggests that such an approach to authorising only unavoidable and reasonable absences, leads to parents who are less likely to offer inadequate explanations and to increased rates of actual attendance.

THEMED STUDY 2
PUNCTUALITY AND LATENESS

Section 7 of the Education Act 1996 requires parents to ensure that their child receives 'efficient, full-time education, either at school or otherwise'. This raises key questions about the definition of 'full-time' and the way in which schools record the data relating to children whose punctuality is poor. In a classic case, Hinchley v. Rankin (1961), it was established that late arrival could still be seen as absence. But many schools have yet to develop coherent policy on this issue and many operate inconsistent or unclear procedures. Since this case, further complications have been added by the creation of authorised and unauthorised absences. The fact that some children now travel long distances rather than attending their local school is also a factor.

Some kinds of lateness may be acceptable, such as those due to an early morning medical appointment, adverse weather conditions or traffic delays. Schools need to make a clear distinction between those late arrivals that are legitimate and those that are not and show that distinction in the attendance register by use of different codes. It must be the school governors and staff, not the parent or the pupil, who define what attendance times are appropriate. Clearly there is room for some discretion to take account of individual circumstances, but unacceptable lateness must be classified as 'unauthorised absence' if LAs are to use such failure as evidence for a Penalty Notice or prosecution. Late arrival which the school has accepted as reasonable cannot then be used against the parent, only as a potential disciplinary issue.

It is the responsibility of each school for children of compulsory school age to define in its attendance policy what the expectations are. Clearly such expectations should also be widely published and reinforced, both to staff, parents and pupils. There must be consistency across the school or there is little chance of developing a whole-school identity on the issue. Differing expectations will confuse parents and make legal action unnecessarily arbitrary. Granted that the lateness is not accepted by the school as reasonable, the key issue concerns whether or not the child arrives during or after the period of time at the beginning of the session which is set aside for registration. (If afternoon registration is not at the beginning, a child must be counted as present if they are there when the register is called no matter when they arrived). Schools are free to decide how long the registration period lasts depending on their circumstances, but it cannot be open-ended or last for the whole time the school is open.

For example, a primary school serving a local area where most children live within walking distance might decide that an arrival time of no longer than 10 or 15 minutes is reasonable in order to be 'on time'. A school where children travel from a wide area and where the problems of traffic and public transport might reasonably come into play could allow longer. The courts have historically indicated that 30 minutes could be seen as a reasonable maximum. Afternoon registration times could be considerably shorter. Once the period of registration is defined, unacceptable arrival outside these times could constitute absence and could therefore be used as evidence, provided such lateness is classified by the school as unauthorised. There might, however, be some individual children where the school wishes to reward the fact that they have come in at all. If so, there is discretion to class any arrival as 'within the registration period', but this should not be a blanket policy.

The attendance register should make it clear which kind of lateness it is. For example, child A is not present when his name is called, so an N is entered. He arrives, however, before the end of the time set aside for registration. The child can now be credited with an attendance and counted as present L. This is not to say that no effort should be made to encourage them to attend a little earlier, but the parents cannot be said to have failed in their legal duty in this situation. The longer the school allows for legitimate registration of this kind, the greater the freedom being accorded to parents. Child B, however, also absent when the register was called, arrives mid-morning without reasonable excuse; well after the registration period has ended. It is important to show that this child is now on the premises after some signing-in procedure (for fire safety purposes etc.), but this late arrival *cannot normally be counted as a legal attendance. This session must be counted as unauthorised absence U. Anything other than an occasional example should be the subject of information to the parents, making it clear that such late arrival is no different from no attendance at all and that legal action could be taken against them on this basis.*

This does raise some practical difficulties. In the short-term, these procedures will increase the number of unauthorised absences and might be seen as reflecting badly on the school. They are likely to lead to greater conflict with parents if standards have previously been unclear. But it is impossible to see the lateness as a problem one minute but count it as a legitimate attendance the next. Parents would rightly ask why they are being pestered if the child's record still shows the lateness as acceptable attendance. Hopefully, in the longer term, a stricter line on punctuality will lead to improvements. These requirements may also lead some parents and pupils to suggest that there is no point in coming in at all if half a session is not to be credited as an attendance. However, it might equally be said that there is no point in arriving on time if coming in at any time is still counted as present. This is most unfair on all those pupils and parents who do ensure that they are there when the register is marked. A suitable balance between these competing principles has to be struck and which still takes account of the fact that a particular child's circumstances might be out of the ordinary.

Given this pastoral discretion, practice within the school should be as clear and consistent as possible. If schools have never indicated in writing to parents and pupils what the expectations are, they cannot be expected to conform to them. If rules are inconsistently applied, an unclear signal will be sent. If schools wish their pupils to attend on time, and if parents who fail to make sure they do so without reasonable excuse are to be identified and challenged, there must first be attention to these issues before action by the LA can be considered as a possibility.

FREQUENTLY ASKED QUESTIONS ABOUT MARKING REGISTERS

Must there be an entry for every half-day session?

Yes, for every pupil of compulsory school age. If it has been agreed that he/she is only required to attend school part-time, there must be an authorised absent mark, (or one denoting attendance at an alternative educational activity), for all the other sessions. There can be no blanks.

Can the same class register be marked by different people?

Yes, provided they all use the same system!

Can the mark in a register be changed?

The legal requirement is that the original mark must still be seen. Computerised systems record when the change was made and who made it. A register is like a birth certificate and can only be altered in this way. Both marks must still be visible.

Do schools have to produce their registers when asked to do so by the LA?

For maintained schools, yes. Academies and other schools may choose to do so. All schools must make information available in response to any child protection enquiry and for use in the Courts. Actual registers as well as the overall statistical data must also be made available for inspection by Ofsted if requested, if, for example, there is a query over the school's procedures.

Who decides whether an absence is authorised?

The school, according to its internal procedures. Advice may be sought from the LA, information may be requested from parents, doctors and others, but only the school *decides* whether or not to accept the explanation. This is essentially the headteacher's responsibility, acting in accordance with policy agreed by the governors but it may be delegated to other staff.

What if there is a doubt about the parent's explanation?

Don't authorise the absence without seeking further information first. Of course it is possible for parents and pupils to try to mislead, but if there is any doubt, leave the absence unauthorised, at least in the short term. This is especially important if the parent is frequently providing trivial explanations for regular absences or if the grounds given do not seem to merit the length of time away. Parents can be asked to provide independent verification of sickness and appointments, for example, but doctors may charge for this and it will not normally be possible for routine minor illnesses. Some parents and doctors are willing to make agreements that designated school staff, school nurses or LA officers can check whether a child has been seen at the surgery, within the limits of confidentiality about the exact reasons. In exceptional cases, doctors may be willing to give an opinion on whether the child is fit for school or how long they should be absent, without actually breaking confidentiality about the cause if that is an issue.

Does the school have to accept the parent's note?

No. The information provided by parents is to help the school decide. It can be ignored if the note does not provide a reasonable explanation. The school should keep all notes if there is any possibility of prosecution. They can be produced in evidence if they provide trivial explanations (or they could be requested by the defence if the parent claims that the child was absent for a legitimate reason which should have been authorised).

Do explanations from parents have to be in writing?

There is no power to insist on written explanations, but telephone messages are more open to misunderstanding. If there are no notes, there could be problems later if there is a dispute. Best practice is for the parent to contact the school by phone on the first day of absence, then to keep in regular contact with the school and to send a note on the child's return. This also guards against the possibility that the child may be staying away without the parent's knowledge. The note must be from the parent/carer for the child unless the circumstances are exceptional, (like a parent who cannot write, understand English or a temporary alternative carer).

What about absences for minding the house or looking after brothers and sisters?

These would not normally be grounds for authorising absence, though in an emergency such as the parent's illness or where the child has on-going caring responsibilities due to parental disability, special pastoral arrangements might be acceptable. The aim should always be to have the child in school as much as reasonably possible.

What about day trips with parents?

These should not normally be authorised as 'leave'. It might be reasonable to allow the odd exceptional day to be authorised for the child who has otherwise attended satisfactorily, though some schools do not grant leave at all for these purposes. While any occasional days taken without permission should then be marked as unauthorised absences and may spoil the child's otherwise excellent record, there is little that can be done about them legally if they are only an isolated event. But if the school rewards 100% attendance, missing out on this achievement might act as sufficient encouragement not to do it.

Why can children have time off for professional modelling, TV, shows etc?

These requests are becoming more common when children are needed for filming, advertisements, shows, professional sports training etc. in school time. This whole area is covered by the Children (Performances) Regulations 1968 and school staff should *always* check whether an LA licence is required before authorising any absence. Absence just to attend TV programmes in school time as a member of the audience, and any activity which will not require a licence, is all at the headteacher's discretion. Professional work must all be licensed but amateur productions are usually exempt. There is no longer any legal maximum for how many days the child can work or how many absences they can have. Any extended absence should require the parent or the person supervising the child to make alternative educational arrangements, such as a tutor.

What about part-time jobs and work experience during school time?

Absence can never be authorised for a child of compulsory school age to be employed in school time. Any information about illegal working should be reported to the LA for further investigation. (This includes Y11 pupils who may seek to work on school days during study/examination leave before the official leaving date). Commercial employers must have a licence to employ even their own children. Children on work experience must be in their final two years of compulsory education and the placement must be approved and supervised by the school under whatever arrangements apply locally. There is no defined limit to how much work experience a child may have and for some children it may be entirely in their interests to pursue this option. One week is probably the norm where it is still offered, but longer arrangements or a regular day a week is legal. Work experience is an 'approved educational activity' (i.e. present), as long as it safe, has been agreed by the school and the pupil actually attends.

Must a child be given a day off for a religious festival?

Yes, schools must grant leave on request. This is one of the specific exemptions in the Education Act 1996 and it applies, of course, to all festivals celebrated by their parents, whatever the religion. However, requesting a day off each Friday for example, is not considered reasonable.

What about a traveller child who only attends now and then?

If the child is currently resident locally they should be in school like any other child, (unless alternative provision has been agreed). However, the Education Act 1996 allows a child to be absent if genuinely away travelling with their parents, provided they attend at least 200 sessions in twelve months (about half time). This should not be used to allow a traveller child to have time off automatically. If the child is registered at more than one school they can be dual-registered both to avoid the absences and to make sure they continue to receive an education. Close liaison should take place with the relevant Traveller Education Support Service for your area if there is one.

What is a 'persistent absentee'?

This is the term used by the DfE to identify those pupils whose absence over the whole school year is below 85%, whatever the reason for the absences. All children at risk of falling into this category, or who are already there, should have an Individual Attendance Plan to encourage improvement and which is subject to regular review.

How do we mark after-school activities?

These are not currently part of the defined school day and so are voluntary. No legal attendance record is required and parents cannot be required to send children to these sessions.

When should a permanently excluded pupil be taken off the register?

Only at the *end* of the exclusion process, including any appeal to the Independent Panel, not on the actual day of the exclusion. As with all fixed-term exclusions, the attendance register should still be marked for each session until then. If nothing else is provided, E counts as an authorised absence. Attending alternative provision should be counted as an attendance, (and must be provided by the LA from the 6th day until the end of the process).

Can all Y11 pupils be given study leave after Easter?

Only if it helps to raise their attainment which may be unlikely! This is authorised absence, not an approved educational activity, as it not supervised and may not actually be used for studying. The DfE has been trying to shorten this period to only the examination period itself, not beforehand or afterwards as well. The school must offer an alternative; parents cannot be required to keep their child at home. All Y11 pupils must receive a mark for each session up to and including the last Friday in June; no-one can leave school before this date.

Can I remove a pupil of compulsory school age from the registers because they've stopped attending?

Only if they have physically moved away, (or after four weeks if their whereabouts are unknown), and in consultation with LA, not just because they haven't attended for any specified period. Parents cannot 'forfeit their place' through their child's non-attendance at any state-funded school (including academies). Neither can they simply remove the child without indicating what other educational arrangements they are making. Removing the child from the registers means they are no longer 'absent' so no legal action can therefore be taken against the parent. There is also a danger that the pupil may be lost to education altogether.

What do I put in the register if it snows and half the children didn't come in?

If the school is closed to all or specified groups of pupils, no marks need be entered in the register for them at all other than 'Y school closed' so the sessions will not be counted, provided their non-attendance is considered reasonable. Those who are expected to attend should still be marked in the usual way. It is important to be clear with parents whether or not the school is open in the event of bad weather or some other problem like frozen pipes or a flood.

What about pre-school children and sixth formers?

The authorised/unauthorised system only applies to children of compulsory school age. For other age groups registration simply records when the child/young person is on the premises. Parents cannot commit an offence in relation to these children.

CHAPTER 4

MANAGING ATTENDANCE

GENERAL

If a parent was thinking of sending their child to your school, or an Ofsted inspector wanted to be assured that the teachers took the attendance of children seriously, where would they be able to see the evidence? Policies are important; management evaluation criteria have their place; (this chapter contains models of both), but the real business of encouraging children to attend is done through personal relationships, hard work and imaginative and stimulating teaching and learning. What goes on in the classroom, or in the corridors, is potentially as important as what goes on at home. Children, and their parents, need to encounter the promotion of good attendance as part of their daily participation in the school. It is not good practice just to leave it as an unspoken assumption until there is a problem.

This is a relatively new emphasis on the importance of what happens in schools. Because the LA, rather than headteachers or governors, hold the legal power of enforcement, there has sometimes been an assumption that Education Welfare Officers (EWO) or other LA managers were ultimately responsible for the levels of school attendance. It was also true that the government historically gathered its information via the LA rather than directly from schools. This sometimes included leaving LA officers to be the bearers of bad news when a school had been identified for additional support or when someone had to be held to account, rather than communicating directly to individual schools themselves. But in general schools are now the drivers of their own destiny, in this area as in others.

Data right down to pupil level is now submitted directly via the School Census, each term and annually. This enables detailed analysis and feedback on an individual school's registration practice to be given. Guidance is addressed directly to headteachers and governing bodies as well as to LAs. There is a clear expectation from Ofsted that Senior Leadership Teams (SLT) should have a clear grasp of what is happening in their school and a coherent plan of action in response, as part of the judgments on 'Behaviour and Safety' and 'Leadership and Management'. Inspectors will expect the school to know what its absence issues are, to demonstrate how it is addressing them and, crucially, to be able to evidence that its interventions are working. All schools benefit from open discussion about attendance and from drawing up clear policies that promote and encourage it. There must at least be an annual process for setting whole-school and specified group attendance targets and evaluating progress. But action needs to be based on an accurate understanding of the issues. The main purpose of this chapter is to help the reader to carry out a review of what is happening in their school and to identify areas that require a strategic response in order to support their pupils more effectively. The primary focus at this point is on the routine and 'normal' situations, not on those that are more complicated or which require more substantial individual or multi-agency pastoral action, (see chapters 5 and 6).

Attendance is not as prominent in the Ofsted Framework as it used to be, though it is still there. Behaviour is certainly more significant in the overall judgment. Only 'Inadequate' for Behaviour and Safety' contains a description; there is no attendance evidence included in the descriptor for 'Good' or 'Outstanding'. Attendance no longer has its own rating; neither are schools compared with schools with similar level of Free Meals as used to be the case. There is simply a comparison with *all* schools and those in the 'bottom 10%', or where trends are going in the wrong direction, are likely to be asked explain what they are doing about it. This may appear to reduce its significance, but I would strongly argue that no school should be worried about attendance in order to please an occasional inspector. Attendance matters because of the children; they have a right to their education and we should always do everything we can to make it happen, even if parents are reluctant to work with us. But sometimes it is schools (and LAs) that let children down. This issue is not all about 'fixing families'. Research has constantly shown that schools can, and do, make a difference.

This emphasis on identifying the 'worst performing' schools might lead some schools, already performing above the average or with few chronic or persistent absentees, to conclude that they have already made sufficient progress. But there will almost certainly be room for some further improvement, however modest. The overall attendance targets should be seen as a *minimum* expectation. They must be communicated to all staff, agreed by governors and constantly monitored. There is not much point in identifying a target if no-one knows about it and without a strategy for hoping to achieve it.

- Has anyone analysed patterns of absence or observed day-to-day registration practice? This often reveals surprises such as the amount of holiday leave, (which may actually be less than is sometimes assumed), particular classes that are quite different from others in the same year group or a teacher who is using a completely idiosyncratic marking system that is understood by them alone!

- Do colleagues recognise the range of reasons given why children miss school rather than just calling it all 'truancy' as has been fashionable in recent years? Which are most relevant where you are?

- What do you understand as the actual *causes* of the absence problems that are characteristic of your individual school, behind the surface 'explanations'?

- What evidence is this analysis based on and what are you doing about it? Various audit tools are available to assist with this process and which the LA should ideally make available if you need them.

- Is there clarity about who is responsible for what? Multi-disciplinary working is essential but the greater the number of partners involved, the greater room there is for confusion.

Everyone, including teaching and non-teaching staff, LA officers, governors, parents and children, will be more effective if they know what they are supposed to do.

- Do people have unrealistic expectations of each other? Is there a clear lead from the governing body and SLT? These expectations are all best defined in an annual school Attendance Plan which is subject to regular management review.

- Are those whose attendance is slipping quickly identified? Consistently-applied procedures that avoid rushing to an immediate judgment about the assumed cause will be essential, especially in large schools.

- When new pupils and parents come into the school, where is the evidence of everyone's commitment to promoting attendance? Is the issue raised at parents evenings and clear, written procedures given out?

- Is there effective liaison with feeder schools, identifying in advance those pupils likely to need additional support and supervision?

- Does the school's website give up-to-date information about attendance, punctuality etc.

- What does the school do to encourage parents and children to attend, especially those known to have a problem, or where there have been difficulties with other children in the family before?

- Have the parents and pupils been consulted over what rewards and incentives might be helpful? How are local industry, commerce, colleges and the community involved? This has to go right down to every child faced with the temptation of staying away today. What will they miss out on if they do? What's in it for them? Sanctions alone are less likely to be effective and may make things worse if they create an even wider gulf between home and school.

- Is partnership just a catchphrase or are there real attempts to make it a reality, especially with the 'difficult' parents and pupils? Think about your own experiences as a parent in other schools; what is it like to be an education consumer? What shortcomings have you encountered as parents or what good ideas could be imported? It is so easy to see things only from the school's point of view.

- What opportunities are there for the pupils to draw attention to issues that might be important in determining their attendance, from bullying to poor teaching? Does the school communicate in ways that all the parents and pupils can actually understand?

Greater ownership of responsibility for attendance is one of the clearest implications of greater local management of schools. The role of the LA is now much more about strategy, co-ordination and specialist support, where it is still involved at all. They should also have an eye to championing children's rights as it is ultimately part of their statutory role to ensure that all children in their area receive an appropriate education. This does not necessarily mean that there will be conflict with a school's own priorities, but an LA cannot be expected always to take the school's 'side' in any dispute. They, at least, must keep an eye on the bigger picture and most schools do still agree to participate in local arrangements, for example, to meet the needs of those children who are 'hard to place'. It will sometimes be tempting to think only of your own school and of the children who are already there. That is entirely understandable. But while we still have a national educational system, *every* child needs to be able to find their place within it. Dealing with absence appropriately is one crucial part of this process.

TOWARDS BETTER PRACTICE

It may be useful to begin with an analysis of the previous year's registers. Computerised systems are now capable of sorting information by the codes used, year groups, gender, even addresses, in order to provide data for subsequent analysis. This might raise a range of issues. Management arrangements should ensure that all staff are carrying out agreed procedures for keeping registers, identifying children with problems, seeking information from parents etc. Too many individuals, each making decisions as they think fit, leads only to confusion.

It is best if staff take the initiative in raising the issue of attendance with pupils and parents. It is evidence of a 'good' school if this role is recognised, even if attendance levels are generally satisfactory. As with bullying or child protection, waiting until a problem arises is not usually adequate preparation for effective action. Parents and children need to see clear signs that the school is committed to promoting attendance; from statements in brochures through to wall displays and classroom work; from accurate information being provided for parents through to prompt action according to clear criteria where a child's attendance is causing concern. Although the government's approach does not always make this clear, it is essential to keep an eye on *overall attendance* as the target, not merely keeping the level of unauthorised absence as low as possible. In the past this emphasis sometimes led to excessive authorisation but there is no longer any incentive for doing this. Without this priority, everyone may settle for a lower level of attendance than could otherwise be achieved. As well as the school's pastoral systems being robust and effective, the curriculum should also be used to raise discussion about attendance and to give pupils an opportunity to undertake their own research. This both raises awareness and may enable the school to act in a preventative way in response to issues identified.

Parents do have a clear legal duty that they should be made aware of and defining expectations is sometimes helpful. But threats of Penalty Notices and even prosecution itself will not necessarily improve the situation if the child or parent feels alienated and disaffected from the school or if there are major problems within the family that are seen as more pressing. Courts are only appropriate for a tiny minority of cases. There will nearly always be an alternative within the school's grasp that is actually more likely to succeed in motivating the child/ parents to improve, though it may need some additional resources and imagination to make it happen. Here especially, thinking 'outside' the box may be essential. Reward schemes for attendance should not involve only those who achieve 100% but be careful to include those who improve and enable those with past problems to get back into the race. The reward has to be attractive, not what the school thinks the child or parent would like. Public recognition, being awarded a certificate in assembly, for example, may be the exact opposite of what would encourage the shy, self-conscious child. Internal 'report card' systems with lesson-by-lesson monitoring; the gaining of stickers or merit points etc may all work with some children but not others. Even older children sometimes appreciate an inter-class competition such as having a cuddly toy as a mascot for the week! Younger children are not so responsible for their own attendance. A prize draw, for example, if you are specifically trying to encourage their parents, might have more appeal if the prize is grocery vouchers rather than a small gift for the child. And you have to be at the attendance assembly to be in it!

Attendance audit/evaluation criteria

The school is actively involved in promoting and improving attendance through the implementation of a policy that aims to achieve agreed annual targets.

Registers are kept in accordance with legal requirements and clear criteria are in place by which absences are authorised or unauthorised.

The attendance policy aims to promote positive relationships with parents and the community.

The policy is regularly monitored and evaluated and targets reviewed to bring it into line, at a minimum, with Ofsted and LA requirements.

A named senior person is responsible for attendance in the school.

There is close liaison between local schools regarding transfer of data about pupils.

A clear pastoral system is in operation within the school in order to maximise links between home and school and other agencies. The role of the LA/EWO (or equivalent), crucial in ensuring good attendance, is clearly understood by all staff.

Initiatives are in place to promote and acknowledge good and improved attendance and to celebrate success in attendance and punctuality.

Pupils are counselled about their attendance and set realistic and achievable individual targets.

Continuity of teaching is encouraged in order to build the child's sense of security.

> *Punctuality throughout the day is monitored and prompt action taken to address problems.*
>
> *The attendance policy lays down clear guidelines to monitor and address internal truancy.*
>
> *The rationale behind good attendance is positively promoted throughout the school.*

It may be helpful to have a general 'home and school agreement' as a way of expressing a joint commitment to improving attendance, but the danger is that they may be seen by some parents and children as setting up them to fail by making impossible demands which they cannot hope to meet. (They do not have the force of law and refusal to sign cannot be used as grounds for removing a child from the school or refusing to admit them). Some parents interpret them only as an attempt to gain evidence against them rather than offering a genuine hope of progress through negotiation and compromise. Setting up so many rules and requirements that the child or parent on the margins is bound to break them, will, in the long run, do little to promote their more positive engagement.

> ### Parenting Contracts for attendance
>
> *Parenting Contracts are a useful resource now available to schools in England. They may be recommended by the LA as a first step in formalising arrangements with parents, prior to considering other enforcement procedures such as a Penalty Notice. Like home-school agreements they are not compulsory or legally-binding, but if a parent refused to co-operate with an offered Parenting Contract and unauthorised absence continues at an unacceptable level, this might be cited later as evidence that the parent has not been willing to address their responsibilities appropriately.*

Model formats should be available locally, but the crucial point about a Parenting Contract is that the school has something to offer to the parent to support and encourage them. For example, a parenting support programme; an opportunity to meet staff one-to-one or work with a parenting mentor in order to raise their skills. There may be resources available in planning such activities, for example, from the Youth Offending Service or local voluntary agencies. Parenting Contracts cannot simply consist of a list of things the parent (or pupil) is required to do. There must also be an offer of help intended to introduce them to new ideas and increase their confidence and parenting capacity.

Schools are free to be flexible about the way they work, within certain limits. But staff, children and parents also need boundaries and to be clear about what they should be doing. Most parents will feel more positive about school if they can see that the school is aware of the needs of the individual rather than simply imposing generalised expectations with no pastoral sensitivity. Written contracts demonstrate that the commitment to seek improvement is genuine. If we are serious about partnership rather than using it as just a slogan to be applied to the 'easy' parents only, agreements and Contracts will have to operate where parents have mental health needs, poor educational achievement and low expectations themselves, different religious or cultural standards etc. Partnership will have to be done differently if the parent cannot read, is a drug user or where the family is undergoing major disruption, but it is needed there more than ever. Progress in improving attendance often breaks down because it was never a remotely equal commitment; the school, parent or child may feel coerced. It may never be truly equal but, for example, parents should not be blamed for what they cannot change; schools must accept that they could sometimes be part of the problem as well as part of the solution.

Attendance casework stages

'Attendance Action'

All pupils below 85% attendance (or hitting interim measures) are identified. Key staff are aware of the need to monitor and promote their attendance. Advice is sought from EWOs or other attendance specialists in school. Each pupil has an Individual Attendance Plan with a named 'supporter' and which identifies targets, relevant issues and strategies for improvement. Parents are offered a Parenting Contract with the school. Clear written criteria exist for the authorising of absences. Warning letters are sent by the school. Regular monitoring and review of progress takes place.

'Attendance Action Plus'

All of the above plus: professionals from outside the school are consulted and involved, ideally using the Common Assessment Framework. A 'Level 2' Parenting Contract is offered that includes additional support by the LA and other professionals as well as the school. More formal warning notices and letters are sent by the LA. Consideration is given to changes in provision. Absences are left unauthorised unless deemed 'unavoidable' by the school. Parents are expected to attend 'Attendance Panels or other meetings with staff or governors.

'LA Action'

All of the above plus: formal referral is made to the LA/Education Welfare Service. Absences are left permanently unauthorised in order to ensure the collection of evidence. Parents are placed under Notice of Caution. Consideration is given to the use of Penalty Notices and other legal enforcement.

No school, unless it selects all of its intake and acts ruthlessly when there are problems, can hope to achieve 100% of possible attendances, but many could do much better. All staff should be conscious of what has been agreed as the school's written strategy. Promoting attendance is not essentially about figures in returns or 'league-table' positions; it is about children, their personal educational and social outcomes and their entitlement to education. Identifying these emphases as the priority, and planning realistic means of ensuring them, are both essential if progress is to be made.

THEMED STUDY 3
OVERCOMING PARENTAL INDIFFERENCE

The world of government publications for parents in which everyone appears to work happily together to promote children's best interests, may not always match the reality. Parents may have all kinds of rights, but some choose not to exercise them, some do not know how to do so and some interpret such language as entitling them to behave as they wish. Schools have all kinds of duties but some operate by informal assumptions and explicit self-defences that may effectively exclude large numbers of parents from participation. Such experiences lead only to frustration all round; to a 'drawbridge' mentality, across which schools and parents view each other with ever-increasing suspicion. The attendance and achievement of vulnerable children may then slip easily down the gap!

Parents who had bad experiences when they were at school may assume that the same attitudes apply equally to their own child's teachers. There will be issues of class, language, race and gender that create barriers in the eyes of some parents. Some may feel reluctance or aggression at the very suggestion that they visit the school, come to a meeting or speak to a teacher. Some will shout at you if they do come because school feels like a foreign country. It is also possible that, in an age of competition between schools, certain families may be seen as detrimental to the school's image and there could be little incentive to try and meet their needs.

There are several contexts in which such misunderstandings may occur:

Attendance

Not all children attend school regularly. Some never do anything regularly; their lives are full of disorder and chaos. Their family may not plan ahead, or be able to anticipate problems. They may be juggling incompatible expectations, of which going to school is only one. It may be only the children who are expected to get up and out by a given time in the morning. Going to school most of the time, or only a little bit late, may to them seem perfectly acceptable. Telling a parent that their child's attendance is 80%, for example, may be interpreted by them as a considerable achievement and nothing to worry about. 80% in anything to do with school was only ever a distant hope when they were there. Any approach to situations like these will require sensitivity, understanding and, above all, flexibility, alongside trying to reinforce the school's reasonable expectations. Giving the family a choice between all or nothing simply creates conflict. If parents are to be helped to see that education is important, they will need to be offered solutions to the other problems that are getting in the way. Threats just add more problems. Try asking yourself questions such as: 'Why should these parents feel positive about school? What is the child missing? What are we offering? What stops them responding?' Maybe 50% of what the school wants is acceptable at the moment, together with other strategies to try and move things along in the longer term.

Letters home

Some parents cannot read English, or not at the level at which letters are pitched. They may ignore anything that looks official. There may be too many circulars sent home. How do parents know which ones are important? Does the school recognise the need for minority languages and simple sentences? Some letters are unclear in what they want the parent to do, or present them only with ultimatums or criticism.

Try imagining what it's like to receive a letter:

- *asking you to come to school to discuss your child's behaviour or poor attendance, (when you've just come out of psychiatric hospital or split up from your partner),*

- *asking for money for the school fund or giving details of the school's skiing trip, (when you're living on reducing benefits),*

- *informing you that your child has been excluded, (when you're trying to hold down a job and don't know how you will cope when he's at home all day).*

If it can be avoided, nothing important should ever be conveyed by standard letter. Some parents may be only five minutes' walk away but no-one from the school has ever knocked on the door. Can what you want to say be said in person, and then written down in way that the parent understands and which takes account of their views as well? Can the communication be both ways, rather than being seen as simply requiring the parent to respond to what the school has initiated? If parents don't respond to letters, find out why- there may be something wrong with the letter.

Parents' evenings

Parents have a right to meet with their children's teachers. However, some dread the idea. This may because they don't want to hear bad news (especially in front of other parents), because they think they'll get 'told off' as they were by their own teachers, or because school is an intimidating and alienating place that isn't for the likes of them. Often parents' evenings offer little confidentiality, no clear purpose to why parents and children are meeting and a lot of waiting or frequent repetition. It is probably better for parents to see fewer staff for a longer time than to hang around for a whole series of quick appointments. It is always worth considering the provision of refreshments, displays, musical entertainments etc. to make the evening more enjoyable. Try to arrange parents' consultations at a time when parents can best attend – early evening can be a very inconvenient time for parents with small children; later might be better, or it might be possible to arrange a creche. Target-setting days, (the DfE does not approve of them!), may exclude those parents who do not have the freedom to leave work so it may be worthwhile offering alternative times to meet. A few parents might even need the teacher to go to them instead; time well spent if it's important to meet.

'Absent' parents

Increasing numbers of children don't live with all those entitled to be involved in their education. Some parents are strangers to the school, live elsewhere and just turn up unexpectedly or are the focus of conflict with their former partner or the child. Parents can feel very hurt when important decisions are made without them or when they have never been told of the child's attendance record, for example. Many parents dismissed as uninterested may not be aware of what's going on. They weren't invited to the meeting, sent a copy of the report or given a chance to take part. They might not be interested, but don't just take the other parent's word for it. Someone in every school needs to have a working knowledge of the Children Act 1989 and its definitions of 'parental responsibility', in order to ensure that parents living apart from their children are treated appropriately. Some will need special opportunities to visit the school outside the normal times or to receive more than the usual information by post.

There are plenty of other potential flashpoints; differences in disciplinary and behavioural standards between school and home; disputes about how the child has been treated at school, (made worse if the school has no proper complaints procedure); parents with a mental illness, learning difficulties or with alcohol and drug problems; times when the school has to take a critical view and when the parent is clearly in the wrong which will need careful handling. However, so much depends on the kind of climate created; whether parents feel part of the school or not. That will make more difference than almost anything. If they are seen as a 'problem' from the moment they walk through the door things are bound to go wrong almost immediately!

FREQUENTLY ASKED QUESTIONS ABOUT MANAGING ATTENDANCE AND ABSENCE

Why do children stay away from school?

Ask them! There are obviously many different answers to this question and it is always worthwhile for a school to do some research, especially at Key Stages 3 and 4, into what is happening and why. Absences are not all the same. The views of pupils about their school experience is now a key feature of an inspection and will be an increasing element as part of evaluating all service provision intended to meet their needs. (With younger children, the focus is likely to be much more on the parents but there are still ways in which their views can be sought). Children may not be motivated to stay away for the reasons we assume. For example, some research has demonstrated that children tend to be at home, on their own, when staying away from school, or with parents, rather than roaming the streets getting into trouble with others. This is also the experience of most Truancy Patrols who regularly encounter more children out of school with their parents, or not actually required to attend, than genuine 'truants'. The reasons may lie more within the school than we think; perhaps the avoidance of a particular lessons such as PE or a conflict with an individual teacher. Children should not be stereotyped without understanding their individual needs.

Does the child have to leave the premises to 'truant'?

Not necessarily. If the definition includes those children who are not where they are supposed to be at each point in the day, an extended trip to the toilet can become what is sometimes called 'internal truancy'. But no offence is being committed even if the child leaves. The word 'truancy' tends to assume that the child came into school and then left again (and was therefore marked as 'present'), or, that they are missing school without their parent's knowledge and consent. Other terms are better for absences initiated, approved or condoned by parents, (see chapter 5).

What are some of the ways of raising awareness about the importance of attendance?

Think carefully about your target group: the pupils, parents, the local community? A poster competition, for example can reach all three: the children do classroom work on the issues and design the posters; parents can be involved as judges or encouraged to come to an event to launch them; the local community can be asked to display them in shops, community halls etc. Some schools have organised visits from theatre companies or mounted displays that are organised by a different year group each month. Boring letters home that seem to be criticising everyone else are probably the worst way! A school must be prepared to accept that while local media coverage is helpful, it may be necessary to manage the news by releasing success stories and countering headlines like 'Local school admits truancy problem'!

Are absentees children 'in need" or just naughty?

Perhaps in general they are a mixture of the two, but the language of need may be better than automatically seeing them as 'bad'. Many children are testing the boundaries or using school as a natural way of showing their anger towards parents, or even towards themselves. Simply excusing what they do or saying it doesn't matter is not helpful – some parents need to face up to this. Some research has shown that young people are as likely to be the victims of crime while they are out of school as they are to be its cause. Children on the streets are always vulnerable, even if they do not think that they are. There are obvious risks when a parent thinks their child is at school but in fact they are not. Children who attend school irregularly are also children 'in need' under s.17 of the Children Act 1989. This should entitle them and their families to services from local agencies in order to promote their health and development, including their intellectual and social development, both of which may be seriously damaged by prolonged absence.

Why is an Annual Attendance Plan helpful?

It is essential that the *whole school* identifies with certain achievable objectives and then keeps them under review. It is difficult to make progress on all fronts at once. It might be, for example, that the emphasis for this year will be on a particular year group or on reducing the amount of time that children have away for family holidays. This would lead to focused campaigns involving just some of the pupils; a theme for the parent's evening, or the school newsletter. The Plan needs to detail what the objective is, how it will be achieved and how progress will be evaluated. That is what Ofsted will be looking for: 'evidence' and 'impact'.

How many persistent absentees have learning problems?

Probably most of them, though whether this is the result of missed education or the cause of it can be very complicated. It is obvious that a child who has missed a substantial number of lessons cannot simply be expected to step back in again as if nothing has happened. But they may have begun to miss school because they do not understand what is expected of them or because of some un-assessed learning need. The involvement of special needs co-ordinators, support units and teaching assistants will be essential in cases like these. It may even be necessary to disapply the child from the requirements of the National Curriculum or allow a phased build-up to full attendance where coming back full-time after a long absence is unrealistic.

Can we use alternatives to school for disaffected pupils?

There is much greater flexibility in Key Stage 4 than there used to be, though unless the child has an identified special need, this can be more difficult with younger pupils, (see chapter 5). Flexibility is always more likely to bring about an improvement rather than insisting on a child being treated in the same way as everyone else when they are clearly different. Coming in for only part of a session can still be classed as an attendance. This can cause difficulty if some pupils appear to be 'getting away' with something that many other pupils might also like to do, like part-time school or a place in a more informal unit. However, it is essential to keep 'education' as the goal, not necessarily 'school'. Alternative provision, vocational courses, including FE Colleges, (which are available to pupils from 14 onwards in many areas, but not everywhere), will normally require the school to part with any remaining balance of the Age Weighted Pupil Unit (AWPU) on a voluntary basis. LAs only have the power to deduct it where pupils have been permanently excluded. Children should ideally remain on a daily register while they continue to be funded as the school's responsibility though it may be appropriate to transfer responsibility for some of them to the LA.

Is bullying an excuse for absence?

It may not be an excuse, but it is certainly an explanation in some cases and is often quoted by parents in Court. This possibility should always be considered in any casework. In confidential surveys bullying, including increasing incidence of cyber-bullying, regularly emerges as most children's key concern about their safety. Unfortunately, many children are reluctant to admit openly to anxiety about school, including any fear of bullying, for fear of losing face. Equally, some parents immediately allege bullying and refuse to admit that their child may be staying away from school because of some problem within the family which they equally may be too embarrassed and reluctant to disclose. The initial explanation is often not the full story. At least in the early stages, the whole process needs to be as 'blame free' as possible; based on a careful assessment of what is happening for each individual child.

Is contacting parents the same day legally required when children are absent?

No, (unless the child came in and then left, when issues of their safety have to be addressed), but it is certainly best practice. Many schools have a system of 'first day contact' which automatically contacts the parents, including by text, if there has been no explanation already provided, though some parents may come to rely on this and not bother to contact the school themselves. But it is possible that the parent does not know the child hasn't been to school and they will reasonably expect the school to inform them at the first available opportunity. Other schools even make a routine home visit. Obviously these contacts should be initially friendly and understanding, not accusatory and be primarily about encouraging an early return. It is always better to create an atmosphere of vigilance and immediate response rather than giving the impression that nothing is likely to happen and that it will be easy to avoid detection.

How can a child be helped back after a long absence?

Getting this right is essential. Too many children tell stories of being made to feel self-conscious or, even worse, being deliberately embarrassed on their return, for some of them at least not to be true. It is best to keep sending some work home, even for a child who everyone accepts should be at school, and to keep up as many links as possible. Sarcasm and other forms of emotional abuse have no place, even when a child appears to have had no good reason for being away. The individual teacher may not know the whole story; inaccurate rumours can spread remarkably quickly in a school. An encouraging, if generally low-key, welcome is most likely to encourage the child to try coming again tomorrow. The first day back can decide what will happen for weeks afterwards.

Can schools discourage a child from attending without realising it?

The influence of parents and friends is obviously important, but many children report that factors within school are more significant than is sometimes recognised. Children have identified boring lessons and unsupportive teachers as key factors. If, for example, there is peer pressure not to attend or some other more tempting possibility, a child's attendance needs to be reinforced as a considerable achievement. It is sometimes too easy to focus only on the negative. There is nothing more likely to alienate a child than a feeling that it doesn't make much difference to anyone else whether or not they attend and that they never get any praise even when they do things right. If parents give this impression of indifference towards their children it becomes highly damaging if their teachers do it too.

Is it right to reward a pupil for doing what they are supposed to do anyway?

This can be a difficult issue, though it is always worth remembering that there is no legal obligation on children to attend, nor do they receive any reward for coming in the form of wages! There is no reason for them to come, other than the fact that what is on offer at the school is seen by them to be of value. For the hard-working, motivated children this may be sufficient in itself; but the child who knows they are never going to feature very prominently in the school's examination figures, may require something more. There has to be a balance between realism and appearing to act unjustly towards the children who are never any trouble and who come without thought of reward.

---

20 ATTENDANCE TACTICS

Try to avoid half-weeks at school in the planning of INSET days and beginnings and ends of terms. Some parents and children will think it's not worth coming in just for a couple of days. Does the school <u>have</u> to be closed on an election day?

Send work home when a child is sick for more than one day with a minor illness. It might prompt a quicker recovery!

Check that absences are not being recorded where an approved educational activity would be more appropriate. If the child is in a supervised educational setting, they're attending.

Use anonymous data on attendance at school as a theme for numeracy, (percentages, fractions, averages etc.) or literacy (spelling, imaginative writing etc.). This will help the children to see that attendance is about them.

Send targeted parents a weekly report on their child's attendance with a suggestion of a reward from them where it's 100%. Don't forget to include those parents who live apart from their children but who may be seeing them at the weekend.

Remember to invite the parent who works in school hours to any meeting, even if it means having to hold it later, or make sure they get information by post, text or email. Many boys in particular are looking for greater approval from fathers and need them to show an interest.

Put the best teachers in the classes where absence and disaffection are most likely to be a problem, at least for some of the time. Inspiration may work where threats will not.

If a child has an early medical or dental appointment, they can still be counted as present if they come in at the first possible opportunity. Reward the parent's effort in getting them in. Half a session is always better than no session at all.

If children leaving the premises for lunch is leading to problems getting them back in the afternoon, how about employing activity leaders for an hour and keeping everyone busy instead?

Use morning registration to celebrate birthdays, make toast, give out rewards, choose the star of the week etc. Make it feel like you really miss out on something if you're not there.

Always avoid sending children home as a punishment. Think of something else that keeps them in school or in some other supervised educational activity.

Offer individual children an attendance mentor: ideally someone from outside the school, local industry or a former student, who will keep a regular eye on them and support them.

Involve your governors in the attendance strategy or as part of an attendance panel that meets with parents or pupils. If they don't see attendance as at the heart of the school's ethos, you can't expect the parents and children to do so.

If children have to be on a part-time timetable for a short time for health or other reasons, try to avoid whole sessions of absence. Coming in late or leaving early is much better. It still allows them to get a mark for that session which missing it altogether doesn't.

Never give the impression that a child is causing a problem for you and it would have been better if they weren't there! They may decide to stay off tomorrow to avoid the hassle for both of you!

If any current strategy to tackle absence isn't working – change it!

Be vigilant about unreasonable staff absenteeism or punctuality. Poor role models are bound to make things worse. There shouldn't be one rule for the staff and another for the pupils.

Include attendance in assemblies and parents evenings so that everyone hears the same messages.

Be proactive about tackling bullying – the main reason why children say they skip school or pretend to be ill.

Try to get a co-ordinated approach across local schools. Parents get confused and irritated if different schools send out different messages, for example, about term dates, family holidays or what to do in response to routine illness.

What's the WIIFM factor? What's in it for staff, pupils or parents if attendance improves? A bottle of wine for the teacher whose class has the most improved attendance, or an extra "free" next week, might make all the difference!

Don't blame parents, pupils, teachers, or yourself for things that aren't their/your fault. Life is sometimes complicated and we are all just trying to do the best we can. Children make mistakes. Parents fail. Teachers can't do everything.

Never give up. There's a new day tomorrow.

MODEL SCHOOL ATTENDANCE POLICY

Principles

Education is important. Missing school means missing out. Children should be at school, on time and ready to learn, every day the school is open, unless the reason for the absence is unavoidable. Permitting absence from school without a good reason is an offence by the parent that can result in legal action by the Local Authority.

Many children are sometimes ill or unhappy about attending school. Families can be going through unsettled times that can make regular school attendance difficult. Any problems with regular attendance, especially any concerns about possible bullying or learning difficulties, are best sorted out between the school, the parents and the child at an early stage. It is never better to cover up children's absences or to give in to pressure to excuse them from attending. This gives the impression that school attendance does not matter and may make things worse.

Every half-day absence from school has to be recorded by staff at the school as either AUTHORISED or UNAUTHORISED. This is why information about the cause of each absence is always required, preferably in writing.

Authorised absences are mornings or afternoons away from school for a good reason like illness or other unavoidable causes.

Unauthorised absences are those which the staff at school do not consider reasonable and for which no "leave" has been given. These are an offence by the parent and include:

- keeping children off school without a good reason
- truancy before the register has been marked
- absences which have never been properly explained
- children who arrive at school too late to get a mark
- taking holidays that have not been approved by the school in advance

Parents are expected to contact school staff and to work with them in resolving any problems together. This is nearly always successful. If difficulties cannot be sorted out in this way, the school may offer parents a formal Parenting Contract or refer the child to the (Education Welfare Officer) from the Local Authority.

He/she will also try to resolve the situation by agreement wherever possible but, if other ways of trying to improve the child's attendance have failed, these Officers can use legal proceedings if required, including Penalty Notices (fines) or prosecution in the Magistrates Court. Alternatively, parents or pupils may wish to contact the (EWO) themselves to ask for help or information. They are independent of the school and will give impartial advice. Their telephone number is available from the school office or by contacting the Local Authority.

Procedures

The school has a special responsibility to reduce the number of children whose attendance is below 85% over the school year. This adds up to missing almost half a term. These are called "persistent absentees" by the Government, whatever the reason for their absence. Special procedures may be applied to children at risk of falling into this category.

The school applies the following procedures in deciding how to deal with individual absences:

Insert procedures covering times of registration, lateness, what parents should do if children are absent, authorisation procedures (notes etc.), arrangements for requesting exceptional leave of absence, use of Parenting Contracts etc.

If the school issues Penalty Notices on behalf of the LA, the procedures and criteria MUST be explained here.

It is not usually possible for the school to authorise absences for shopping, looking after other children, minding the house, birthdays, day trips etc. Leave may however, be granted on compassionate grounds in an emergency (e.g. after the death of close relative).

Please note that a request for a term-time holiday is NOT a parental right. Leave may be granted in exceptional circumstances but arrangements should not be made without the school's agreement in advance. Taking leave without permission is "unauthorised" absence and can be subject to a Penalty Notice fine or other legal proceedings by the Local Authority.

Parents are asked to make routine medical and dental appointments outside school time wherever possible. Where such appointments in school time are unavoidable, staff should be informed in advance if at all possible. A 'present' mark may still be awarded if the child attends for as much of the session as they can. It is always better to attend for some of the time, rather than missing the whole day.

The school has adopted the following attendance targets and special projects:

Insert information specific to your school about your overall attendance targets, reducing persistent absence and any special strategies and plans

The people responsible for attendance matters in this school are:

Insert information specific to your school

The school has a legal duty to promote good attendance. Equally, parents have a duty to make sure that their children attend regularly. School staff are committed to working closely with parents as the best way to ensure as high a level of attendance as possible. Please work with us.

CHAPTER 5

WORKING WITH PARTNER AGENCIES

GENERAL

All schools have children who are sometimes absent for reasons other than a strictly 'unavoidable' cause. As has been outlined in chapter 4, a great deal can be done by staff, with sensitivity, good organisation and proactive intervention with both pupils and parents, to ensure that promoting good attendance is at the heart of the school's ethos. Most of the time, this range of responses will be sufficient to deal with the school's overall strategic tasks *and* the vast majority of individual children's situations. But for some schools, and for some children, wider and more complex issues are a major element of their absence profile, so rather more will be required. Once low-key support procedures and general pastoral care have failed to resolve the problems, or from very early on in some cases, there may be a need for the school to involve a range of professionals from outside their own teaching staff. Even if the presenting cause is within the school itself, such as bullying, clashes with a teacher or learning difficulties, the impact of the non-attendance may be felt in areas of the child's life well beyond the school and may require action on a number of fronts at once.

Absence from school might have been seen in the past by other professionals as only an 'educational' problem. This may have led them to give such issues a lower priority than schools are required to do. But this attitude is no longer acceptable. If the reasons are medical, emotional or psychological, that makes it a 'health' problem. If the absence is due to parental indifference, that makes it a 'parenting' problem. If the child is caring for a sick relative, that makes it a 'young carer' problem. If the family has broken up through violence or had to move because of some other crisis, it may become a 'housing' problem. If the child is at risk of harm to their health and development, that makes it a 'child protection' problem. If the child commits offences when not at school, it becomes a 'youth offending' problem, etc. A Serious Case Review about the death of a young child while in the care of a teenager who had recently left the 'looked-after' system, was highly critical of agencies for delaying intervention in her desperately neglectful family because the issues were dismissed as 'only about non-attendance at school'. That was, of course, a wholly superficial analysis but by the time action was taken it was largely ineffective in helping her to get her life back on track. Many schools could no doubt tell similar stories.

Defining our terms

The appropriate response to a child's absence obviously depends to a large extent on the nature of the issues involved. So a thorough process of assessment is absolutely essential before attempts are made to address it. There are a number of reasons why a child may be experiencing difficulty in attending regularly, (beyond the minor incidents that are easily resolved). The nature of the absence needs to be carefully analysed in order to know who else should be involved:

'Truancy'

This term is best applied to those children who are absent without the support or encouragement of their parents. This may be for whole sessions or when children leave the school site or absent themselves from lessons, after registering. This is largely a pastoral or disciplinary matter, not a question of law enforcement, best sorted out with the parents and the pupil as soon as it begins to happen. Children do not break the law by such behaviour and may not even be recorded as 'absent'. Even if the Police get involved or if the child is apprehended in the street, there is no offence of 'truancy' for which action can be taken against them. Much can be done by schools to tackle such issues with vigilance, flexibility and imagination. Many children respond to incentives and rewards for improvements but some will not easily do so. Research tends to suggests that behaviour of this kind is more common among girls than boys. (Boys tend to misbehave more and get excluded).

'Parent-condoned absence'

If parents are condoning, colluding with or even actively initiating the absence, this should not be described as truancy. This *is* a legal matter and *persistent* failure to act responsibly by parents may be the subject of proceedings by LA officers, provided the absences remain unauthorised. Schools cannot hope to detect all the examples for which untruthful explanations have been provided, but they must try. This has become a key emphasis in recent years as successive governments have been keen to emphasise that parenthood is more about responsibilities than rights and making sure that their child is in school is fundamental to being a responsible parent. Reminding parents that they do have a legal duty will be an inevitable part of any response to unreasonable absences of this kind, but it also means having to find ways of continuing to work with those parents wherever possible. They will still be there when the Penalty Notice has been delivered or the Court case is over, so rebuilding the relationship will be essential if the action is to be of any lasting value. There is no point blaming the child in situations like these.

'Emotionally-based school refusal'

These children do not attend at all or only very occasionally, sometimes even at more specialist provision. Such refusal is usually an indicator of some deeper problem in the child's personal or family life, including abuse and psychological or psychiatric problems, such as depression and anxieties as well as major emotional, behavioural or learning difficulties. A wide range of professionals and services may be needed including education, social care and health. Estimates suggest that mental health problems can be an issue for one in ten children; over 100 in an average high school. As many as one in six may have experienced either physical or sexual abuse. Many of these children can be helped but a few of them will have chronic needs over long periods. For some, action under the Children Act 1989 or use of the Common Assessment Framework may be appropriate. Special educational provision may be required or alternatives to school such as home tuition, at least in the short term.

'Parentally-based social or emotional difficulties'

It is not only children whose social circumstances or emotional health may affect their school attendance. Parents with drug or alcohol issues; those with learning difficulties and those whose personal domestic situations are unstable, will all find the routines of daily attendance difficult. In situations like these, school staff may need to make contact with the providers of adult services with whom you are not currently familiar. Adult mental health issues are a significant indicator of likely problems with children's attendance. These parents, even if they do not readily respond to the school's concerns, may not necessarily have the anti-social and deliberately unco-operative attitudes that might be assumed from first impressions. People whose lives are in almost constant crisis do not necessarily see the significance of letters, meetings and formal procedures. Threats of enforcement are unlikely to make them more able to respond. Prosecution may even add to their problems and prove counter-productive if there are issues around separation anxiety from the child or not being able to cope with mounting problems without having them at home during the day to support them.

'School-initiated authorised absence'

There are some absences for which neither the child nor the parent can be held responsible. If the pupil is not at school because of exclusion, either formal or informal, or because the initiative in telling them not to attend has been taken by the school, no legal powers can reasonably be used against the parent. If they have been removed from the registers there is no evidence of absence at all.

It is unfortunate that some of these situations, which can lead to children being out of school for long periods, can still be presented as 'unauthorised absence' or even 'truancy' when that is clearly not the case. This seems to be a particular issue for some children with SEN, (who are six times more likely than the general school population to be excluded), or even those considered unlikely to achieve success in GCSEs. Absences such as these can rarely be resolved by the actions of others outside the school, though some may arise because of a perceived lack of support for the school from other agencies that may need to be addressed if such actions are to be avoided.

Key partners in addressing non-attendance:

- *specialists from among the school's own team such as counsellors, the special educational needs coordinator (SENCO) or home-school liaison workers;*

- *education welfare officers, educational psychologists, behaviour support teams and other LA or school-based resources where learning or behaviour issues are significant;*

- *health workers such as school nurses, health visitors, general practitioners, child and adolescent mental health teams and adult community mental health workers;*

- *youth workers, careers advisors and others who work with young people in the local community, including police officers and PCSOs;*

- *family support workers and social workers from the LA's Children's Service who may be able to intervene where there are significant concerns for the child's safety and welfare or a breakdown in their family relationships and the arrangements for their day-to-day care;*

- *the 'Troubled Families Programme' which works very intensively with a small number of families where anti-social behaviour, rent arrears, youth offending etc. have identified them as needing targeted interventions;*

> • *voluntary agencies such as the NSPCC, those working with drug and alcohol abuse or organisations that provide help and advice to children and families, including, for example, young carers and children with specific medical conditions.*

Teaching, pastoral staff and others responsible for this area should seek to develop local contacts with as many colleagues as possible in order to maximise communication and the effective resourcing of support. Teachers often say that they are not social workers and cannot be expected to spend their time sorting out social problems as well as teaching. This is true, and therefore makes it all the more necessary that key school staff build an effective network with others which enables them, hopefully with the support of the child's parents, to make efficient referrals to those who can assist in moving things forward. Many other services for children besides teaching may now be physically based in schools. Some have become 'extended schools', offering a wide range of family support beyond the regular teaching hours. Teaching staff and school leaders must expect to work in partnership with other colleagues as a matter of routine. This sounds so obvious, but it doesn't always seem to happen. How does a child come to be excluded when their social worker or foster carer didn't know there was a problem? How do some children end up with no school to go to? Nearly always because there has not been enough communication with colleagues *before* the action is taken.

This is especially important in dealing with absence. It is a dangerous assumption that a child is having problems attending simply for disciplinary reasons, (by the child or the parent). It has become fashionable to describe not attending as just another kind of deviant behaviour. (I assume that is why attendance and behaviour are now grouped together in the Ofsted judgment, with behaviour by far the dominant element). But things are often much more complicated than that. At its most extreme, for example, the child might be struggling with the consequences of sexual abuse and calling attention to their plight in the only way they can think of. In many more routine cases, involving an outside agency need not be seen as any criticism of the family, though many parents will probably feel guilty about their inability to cope unaided, even if they won't admit it. Some children pose major problems and the last thing a school will want to do is to heap on a further sense of failure in either parent or child if it is inappropriate.

The Common Assessment Framework

The CAF provides a set of shared tools with which professionals can work with families in order to promote better outcomes for vulnerable children. Where problems are identified that require a multi-agency response, someone from the school may be best placed to initiate a full assessment of the child's needs and identify what contribution each agency may be able to make. The Framework creates an opportunity for working with families to produce an initial assessment of the child's needs and the identification of any more specialist services that may be needed, co-ordinated by a 'lead professional' who could be from any relevant agency. This should result in more informed referrals and less of a sense that social workers are the repository of all those children that no-one else knows what to do with! This is now a joint responsibility on all those who currently have any knowledge of the child.

It is not easy to make the CAF work, especially in a climate of rapidly reducing local services. School staff may feel frustrated that their concern does not meet the 'threshold' or that parents will not co-operate. This is entirely understandable but we need to develop both our resilience and our creativity, rather than abandon the agreed procedures. That will rarely create a better outcome. If the system isn't working where you are, make sure that those views are communicated at a senior level. We cannot always make people, parents or professionals, do what we want them to do and they may have a different set of priorities. Schools are entitled to support, but we have to get away from the idea that it will be in the child's best interests for them be passed around like an unwanted parcel!

Neither are truancy and poor attendance associated with youth crime and anti-social behaviour in every case. This is a key concern of government at present, but not all of the rhetoric in this context fits very comfortably with the wider picture of greater support and help for families. People are not likely to seek help if they think they will be blamed. There is a genuine tension in approaches here that schools, among others, have to cope with. It is true that the vast majority of those who end up in Youth Offender Institutions and even in prison have had poor educational experiences, as have many of those in the care of the LA. Undoubtedly failure at school sets a young person onto a treadmill from which it is extremely difficult to escape. This is one reason why it is so important to tackle it at the time. However, this is not to say that a child who is not attending school will *necessarily* grow up to be a criminal or that their poor attendance is automatically a sign of rebellion and hostility to authority and that it should routinely be approached as such.

The Education Welfare Service

Much of this inter-agency context has changed a great deal since 2008; perhaps nowhere more so than here. Where they still exist to provide anything beyond enforcement, Education Welfare Officers should be of particular assistance in these more complex situations. However, LAs do not have to provide any kind of early intervention or voluntary casework service and many have withdrawn to Court work only or, if additional support is to be provided, schools may have to pay for it. If still available in this way, these officers will not want to be seen only as the authority figure that is brought in at the last moment when a whole series of more supportive steps could have been taken first. However, even if nothing else is now on offer, the LA *must* be told of any children who have been absent for two weeks without proper explanation and those whose attendance has been unsatisfactory over a period of time. (Many LAs now use 'likely to achieve below 85% attendance' as an indicator of serious concern, in line with government expectations).

This process should not be left to chance and internal school procedures must include ways of identifying such children and ensuring that they are discussed with the relevant person. Given their growing scarcity, EWOs are increasingly operating in ways that do not necessarily mean that they will take over all the intervention themselves. They are as much responsible for assessment and advice as for direct service provision. Many local service level agreements spell out this role in more detail according to the nature of the arrangement between the LA and the various schools in its area. Academies and free schools, for example, are likely to be charged for all services beyond the statutory which might still be provided at no cost in schools the LA maintains. Any school can, however, purchase such non-statutory services from elsewhere and a number of independent EWSs are now emerging. If so, it is essential that these workers are recognised as part of local inter-agency arrangements. There may also be other specialist or information services available to which the EWO can refer the family.

If the issues are assessed as within the general area of enforcement, having exhausted a range of other strategies, the first step is for the school to make it clear with the parents that the absence is unauthorised. It must be clear that the *school*, not the parents or the child define the status of the absences. A procedure for tightening up the authorisation process will often, in itself resolve the problem. Many parents and children respond well to clearer expectations. If the school has never explained the problem, and has previously responded to unacceptable absence by still authorising it, families will not necessarily see why there is any need to change their behaviour. This is especially important in defining the school's attitude to lateness or when parents are regularly providing trivial explanations for absence. Meetings with parents; governors' attendance panels; Parenting Contracts; written arrangements to clarify authorisation procedures or independent verification that a child is unfit for school, may all enable clearer ground rules to be accepted and progress to be made. EWOs may be able to assist in making these arrangements but there must be a willingness by the school to define the absence as unacceptable by not authorising it. Other kinds of absence will require quite different responses.

The statutory process (see also chapter 2)

Where unauthorised absence persists, despite the efforts of the school and others to work with parents to reduce it, formal referral to the LA for legal intervention will often be appropriate. Schools must know how to access this procedure, especially as many LAs may not now advertise its availability too widely! The school's attendance policy should make it clear to parents that the LA is available to assist them with any problems in ensuring that their children attend regularly, but that they also carry powers of legal enforcement. Clear arrangements should be in place to ensure that the LA has all the necessary information on which to act. Except in a rare emergency, it is beneficial if contact with the LA can be prepared for and timetabled in order to make best use of the time available. Written referrals should be followed up with further sharing of information wherever possible.

Referring to the LA

Standard referral forms should include:

- *Child's full name, date of birth, address, year group, age and ethnic group;*

- *Details of the family situation as known to the school, including, wherever possible, the full names of all those with parental responsibility, together with whoever is living with the child, and whether the family is aware of the referral. They do not have to consent to it but it is helpful to know what they have been told;*

- *A copy of the current register and statistical information relating to the child's record of attendance, including grounds on which any absences have been authorised or left unauthorised;*

> - *What the school has already done (e.g. under 'School Action' and 'School Action Plus') in order to attempt to resolve the problems, including meetings with parents, letters home, Parenting Contracts, contact with other professionals etc.;*
> - *The member of staff responsible for the referral and when they are available for further consultation;*
> - *Space for the LA to report back on the action to be taken and issues identified for further action by school or others.*

In many situations, difficulties are resolved by home visits, casework etc. undertaken by the EWO in partnership with the school. Officers may also make use of group work or other interventions as required. LA officers generally adopt a practical problem-solving approach that attempts to identify the underlying causes of the absence and then to devise strategies to resolve them, but some may be trained in more specialised counselling skills or therapeutic responses. Referral may be necessary to other professionals and agencies as an alternative to legal action where this has not been explored already; changes in educational provision may be recommended to parents and the school. The normal emphasis will be on enabling the parents and child to take action themselves, even if the Penalty Notice or court process is needed to do it, and providing an element of authority and structure which requires the family to confront the absence and do something about it. LA officers have a right to be forceful with parents in a way which school staff cannot. They should not be afraid to challenge parents' explanations where appropriate, even without the power of a Court behind them. If issues concerning the school, such as bullying, exclusions, special needs or study problems are relevant, they may seek to offer independent advice to *both* the school and the family in considering any necessary responses. Flexibility, imagination and increased communication are often the most likely ways in which to bring about improvements.

It may be that a Penalty Notice can be issued for a defined level of unauthorised absence, such as a holiday taken without advance permission, without this full process of prior assessment or perceived need for ongoing work with the family. If this has been agreed as part of the local Code of Conduct then this is a reasonable expectation, (as long as the LA follows through in the event of non-payment), though I personally am not convinced of the usefulness of such a procedure if that's all the relevant absence there is. If this is *not* an isolated issue and where problems persist, LA officers may make use of their own written agreements, or a 'Level 2' Parenting Contract, usually drawn up at a meeting with parents as a last attempt to avoid court action. Of course such agreements are not always possible but they should always be attempted prior to any more formal procedures. Many parents do not respond until the very last opportunity and may find this a helpful way of concentrating their efforts towards specific goals and outcomes, provided they are kept under review and changes made as required. Rewarding children (and their parents) for progress is essential, not just the imposition of greater sanctions should the agreement prove unsuccessful. If use of the Courts is being actively considered, the LA may call a formal meeting which may include placing the parent under a 'Notice of Caution' and use of the Police and Criminal Evidence Act 1984. Key school staff should regard attending these meetings as a priority and they have a vital contribution to make. It is essential not to allow situations to drift with no obvious response.

Statutory enforcement procedures should be used only if they are the best available response to a given set of circumstances, and sufficient evidence exists to secure a conviction, not just because we can't think of anything else! The reason for a prosecution must always be that it is the best available tool to get the child back to school. If that has already happened, or if the action against the parent is highly unlikely to make any difference, then something else needs to be considered. (There may even come a point where the parent enjoys a few weeks in prison in order to escape all their problems for a while!) Prosecutions are time-consuming on everyone involved and not always effective and, wherever possible, other strategies are to be preferred. It may be more likely to work as a threat than as a reality; some families simply do not worry about courts, fines etc. as others do, or it may make no difference at all to the behaviour of an emotionally damaged child. It's like a game of golf. When I am 300 yards from the flag there is no point in picking up a putter, or using a 3 wood when I am on the green 6 feet from the hole. I sometimes wish our thinking in response to absence was equally sophisticated!

THEMED STUDY 4
EDUCATION SUPERVISION ORDERS

Ensuring that children attend school properly is largely a matter of persuasion, encouragement and negotiation. The use of legal powers is bound to be restricted to only a tiny minority of situations where parents have failed to exercise their statutory responsibilities and all reasonable attempts to resolve the problems on a voluntary basis have been tried and have failed. The most frequent Court action by local authorities is to prosecute parents under s.444 of the Education Act 1996 for the offence of failing to ensure that their child is properly educated, on the basis of unauthorised absence only.

Children Act 1989

There is, however, an alternative power under s.36 of the Children Act 1989 that is used much less frequently and is often overlooked as a potential solution. It is supposed to be considered before any prosecution, but this seems to be largely a paper exercise in many LAs. These proceedings are based on total absence, not just on unauthorised absence and could even be applied for in relation to a home-educated child of compulsory school age. On application by the LA to the Family Proceedings Court, the child and their parents can be allocated a supervisor to 'advise, assist and befriend' them and to give 'directions' as to how they should be educated. Such supervisors are normally Education Welfare Officers or senior school staff and their role is to work with the family on a formal basis where their children are not being 'properly educated'. It is worth asking why this provision is so rarely used and whether LAs are failing to make use of all the resources at their disposal.

These applications are linked to other Children Act Orders and require prior consultation with children's social care to ensure they are the correct response to the child's needs. This seems to a problem as many LAs have never agreed an appropriate procedure for making such a decision. The power to apply to the Family Proceedings Court to have a child placed under the supervision of the LA's education service was seen at the time of its introduction as largely a replacement for the previous power to use absence from school as grounds for care proceedings. The general feeling is that they would not work in such a context or that parents have to be co-operative. Both of these are misunderstandings that have tended to obscure the contribution that ESOs might make in the right circumstances.

A child who is refusing to attend school, despite the very best endeavours of his or her parents and professional workers, may, or may not, be 'beyond parental control'. If so, and if such a situation is leading to either 'significant harm' or the risk of it, this may still be grounds for care proceedings as before. The difference, and it is obviously important, is that LA education officers cannot initiate such action as they used to be able to do. Only social workers can apply for Care Orders to obtain 'parental responsibility' for the child and so change where they live etc.

Not attending school, on its own, is unlikely to give sufficient grounds; but this was the case before the Children Act as well. Education authorities never sought Care Orders only because of absence; there were always a range of other risk factors involved. Care proceedings might still be appropriate for children experiencing multiple problems that are putting them at risk of harm, including failure to attend school with the consequent damage to their intellectual and social development. They are, however, rare as social workers do not necessarily have any greater chance of changing their behaviour than does a parent.

The power left to EWOs (or their LA equivalent) is more limited, and not for children in such extreme circumstances. But it is still significant. It is not a power to force a child to go to school, neither is it a punitive approach to either child or parent. It is however, (and many LAs do not seem to see this), a positive opportunity to address the needs of children whose welfare is being threatened because they are missing out on education. The focus is the child's welfare; if that is being compromised there is a duty to seek Orders to address the issues. The 'welfare of the child' is paramount in all work arising from the Children Act. 'Non-intervention' or working by agreement with parents are not more important than the needs of the child. This has been the same mistake as has sometimes been made by those who put partnership with parents above protecting children in child abuse cases.

There is a widespread assumption that either ESOs are not needed (because we can achieve what is required by agreement) or, even if something is needed, ESOs cannot deliver it because they have no 'teeth'. If we can resolve a child's problems without resource to the Courts, this is, of course, preferable. However, there are many children who are not attending satisfactorily, who are not 'beyond parental control' but where a more timetabled, structured and authoritative role for a professional might be of benefit.

Supporting and challenging parents

ESOs are best used when parents are failing to deliver their educational responsibilities towards their child, but not necessarily behaving in a way that justifies prosecution. It may be that absences have been authorised, perhaps on grounds of alleged sickness, but there is a still *a question as to the parent's lack of appropriate action. Any Children Act Order must be 'better for the child than no Order', but since Essex v B (1993), this should present no problem if the intention of the Order is to ensure that the child is 'properly educated'. It is always better for a child to be educated than not to be educated and that will always be the Order's intention. The priority is still on reinforcing the parents' duty, but on longer-term responses rather than a one-off court appearance, a small fine and no change in behaviour.*

It is a mistake to say that parents must be completely co-operative for an ESO to work. No Children Act Order is appropriate unless there is some dispute that needs resolving by the Court. The guidance simply says that Orders are unlikely to be effective if parents are 'hostile'; (prosecution is for that). But there are many points between co-operation and hostility. Parents may be indifferent, disorganised or inconsistent. They may be tacitly colluding with the child's absences rather than confronting them. They may be weak, powerless or lack basic parenting skills. They may have multiple difficulties of their own, including drug and alcohol problems, mental health needs, learning difficulties and physical health issues and be unable to focus adequately on the needs of the child. They may have fully intended to educate the child themselves but are just not capable of doing so and the child is missing out on crucial stages of their development as a result.

There may be no grounds for leaving the absences unauthorised so there can be no offence, but the child's welfare may still be threatened by missing large amounts of education, especially, for example, if the child has special needs. In all these situations, prosecution is certainly a waste of time or even impossible. Establishing a more formal relationship with the family through an ESO may well be much more productive. This emphasis on parents has often been overlooked but ESOs are still a response to parental failure, not driven by the misbehaviour by the child.

Powers of the supervisor

A supervisor has considerable powers, though they will need significant inter-personal skills in exercising them. They can offer advice etc. and should clearly do so. They should be consulting closely with both child and parent about solving the problems; but they can also give written 'directions' to the parent, for example about providing evidence of work done at home, admitting the child to a new school, supporting them while there, or attending meetings etc. Persistently failing to follow such directions is an offence, (though I am not sure anyone has ever been prosecuted for it). The supervisor can also give directions the child; though this may be seen as less useful as the child cannot commit an offence by ignoring them. But if the ESO is not working for this reason, further assessment by social care should take place and any new Orders or applications considered.

Conclusion

No doubt many LAs have failed to make use of ESOs on the grounds that they lack the resources for what will be inevitably time-consuming and costly interventions. Schools will need to recognise that such children will require a disproportionate amount of time if they are to be helped. The active involvement of the child's school is essential if ESOs are to succeed. The supervisor must have the confidence of the headteacher and key staff and there has to be full consultation about any problems, including, for example, any possibility of exclusion or other major change in the child's circumstances that would undermine the intentions of the order. Supervisors effectively become another parent involved in the child's education and cannot hope to achieve success unless everyone is working together.

ESOs are still an untried possibility in many LAs and government has historically given them little prominence, although they are still included as an option in the 2013 'Advice'. They are not a magic wand; nor will they change the unchangeable; but a mythology of difficulty seems to have grown up around them that needs to be challenged.

Given adequate resources, they might make a real difference to some children and prevent problems from reoccurring later because no real change has been effected. Perhaps before we search around for other ways of dealing with children's attendance problems, and introduce yet more legal powers and interventions, it might be as well to make better use of the all the options that are currently available.

THEMED STUDY 5
ALTERNATIVES TO SCHOOL
Alternative provision

I don't personally like this term as it immediately suggests something of lesser status and value than a school – I prefer the term 'appropriate provision – but I'll use it because everyone else does. Although an Ofsted report in 2013 indicated that many are not doing it properly, LAs have the power to arrange education outside school for children, including those who are having attendance or behaviour problems. Very ill children, for example, who cannot manage a full day at school may receive some part-time tuition in hospital, in a specialist centre or even at home. If no other provision is made and they are still on a school register, as most will be, that may generate considerable numbers of absences, which will be counted against the school, which seems most unfair given the unavoidability of the situation. I once heard a government spokesman say that every child should be in school every day but that's clearly not realistic given the circumstances of some of them.

Some children will end up in a Pupil Referral Unit which, at their best, will provide them with a range of educational opportunities that might not have been available in their school. These may include practical skills and trades, as well as an opportunity for catching up on basic literacy and numeracy which is often a huge obstacle to their attendance in a mainstream setting. Indeed, many PRUs end up having to operate as unofficial special schools for children with learning, emotional and behavioural difficulties which have not been properly addressed before. (If more frequent testing will stop this happening then I'm all for it, as long as those who need the extra help are there when the test is taken!)

PRUs do not have a particularly good reputation and governments are constantly talking about the need for reform of this kind of provision, though this may simply be about re-establishing them under another name or with new forms of governance. Some guidance documents suggest that they should be able to meet the same standards as schools in terms of attainment and attendance. That strikes me as wholly unlikely, unless they admit only children who don't really need to be there. Schools can, of course, make their own temporary 'off-site' arrangements, but they will find exactly the same problems continue unless it is very different from what is usually available, and this will often have already been tried before we get to this point.

There is an increasing drive to bring in new provision from outside the LA, though cost is often an issue if they are seeking to make a profit. There is undoubtedly scope for more competition and innovation of this kind but it's not always clear who should take responsibility for making sure it happens. LAs are no longer necessarily considered the best way in which to do this, so more of this commissioning role must fall to schools doing it for themselves, ideally in partnership with each other and external providers. I would like to see far more effort made to find good quality, monitored and accountable provision for their pupils, rather than settling for a 'one size fits all' approach, but there is little incentive to do so.

I think we just have to accept that not everyone must still be linked to a school in order to receive an appropriate education, and that it cannot always be full-time. Schools should not have the market all to themselves. New small-scale facilities which avoid many of the negative associations of 'school' may stand a much better of chance of success with some young people and their families. They may be able to operate outside the conventions and constraints of the normal school routine and can be more relaxed about hairstyle, language, clothing, mobile phone use etc. These can seem like very minor issues but they are major irritants to mainstream schools and the source of considerable conflict. Even something like smoking, to which some teenagers are undoubtedly already addicted, may be enough for a conventional school to be out of the question. Does it necessarily have to mean that they can't therefore be educated at all?

Many would argue that this is just giving in to unacceptable behaviour, but given some of these children's past circumstances, getting them to engage in any kind of structured learning at all is surely far more important? I don't expect most schools to be able to show the degree of flexibility required to provide it all themselves. So we have to find a way of paying for it in a way that doesn't leave them sitting on an entirely nominal school register where a row of B codes may not tell the whole story.

e-learning

There are national programmes such as 'Not School' and 'Ed-lounge', as well as arrangements made by LAs, that enable a young person to study an IT-based programme, either at home or in a support centre. I have to admit that I am not a great fan of this approach if used in isolation, but if it is the only way to interest them in some kind of supervised and supported programme, then it may be worth considering. 'Not School', for example, operates by installing restricted-access computer equipment in the child's home and then providing them with both accredited packages of learning and on-line live tutorial support, often at times when schools would not be available.

No face-to-face teacher contact is involved at all. Interestingly, much of the work, done when the young person chooses, is done and submitted to on-line mentors late at night. The timing of the school day may be a key obstacle to their participation in conventional provision. (There have been one or two experiments with a later start and finish for secondary schools, though all schools still have to have 2 sessions. The current structure is something we have inherited from the C19th which may no longer always be fit for purpose for some of those for whom it is intended).

Like many others, perhaps particularly of my generation, I don't much like this way of learning when I have to use it myself. But given that something very similar is involved in passing the driving theory test and much Level 1 child protection training is now delivered in this way, it must have some merit. It doesn't have to be used exclusively of course and could be combined with other opportunities. If the alternative is just more nagging about not being in school or repeated legal action which produces no useful end result, it must be worth considering.

One group who might particularly benefit from this approach are some looked-after children in local residential units, most of which will these days be run by external agencies and private sector organisations. This is often a very disaffected group, for whom prosecution of their parents is impossible because we are their parents now! Looked-after children should ideally be in a school; and most are. But a few older children in particular have had such damaging experiences that such a regular routine is impossible at present. They have professional staff available to them 24/7 so perhaps time spent working on an e-learning package together, if only on an interim basis, will not only help the young person educationally but also provide a useful opportunity for the child/adult bonding that some so desperately need.

Work works!

I have been arguing for years for reform of the laws on child employment. They are hopelessly out of date – the core legislation still in use dates from 1920 and 1933! As a result, most children and young people who work do so illegally, but not necessarily inappropriately. Only a fraction will have the supposedly required license from the LA, but most of it still goes on uneventfully. Given that the rules apply until the end of Year 11, even if the young person is well past their 16th birthday by then, they are often seen as irksome and irrelevant by all concerned. What I am interested in here is whether the work that many children and young people do anyway could be seen in a more positive light as part of their 'education', either as well as, or even instead of, going to school, at least for a while. Work has traditionally been seen as a threat or an interference with school. Again, that strikes me as an outdated assumption that needs to be challenged.

Even some of those who are not attending school might still be holding down a part-time job. The response to this situation is usually to try to take it away from them. If they can't get to school as well then it's the job that has to go, though local authorities can only do that if they have issued a license in the first place, which they often haven't. I can understand the logic, but I can't really see the point of removing the one thing about the young person's life that suggests they do still have some self-respect and reliability. That kind of thinking might seem fair, but is just too rigid for creative solutions to become possible. The chances are they will be even less likely to go school, if only out of spite and to wind up those who have taken away what might have been an essential source of income for themselves or their family. And there is, of course, absolutely no guarantee that they will not immediately get some other more unsuitable job and just keep quiet about it.

I'm not just saying that anything goes. If the job they have isn't safe or is specifically illegal we will have a problem, at least until we get some relaxation of the rules, which must surely happen eventually. But the magic words are 'work experience'. This enables young people to get a taste of the world of work, even in school hours, and in settings that are not necessarily where they can be 'employed'. That's what it's for. No-one ever had a work experience placement delivering papers! Most Key Stage 4 pupils get some kind of brief work experience, but we could make much more of it for those who are so turned-off by school. They'd have to turn up and do it of course, but many might do so if we *can find something that interests them. Perhaps an 'allowance' can be paid instead of wages. Of course it won't always make a difference but all these kinds of options are much more likely to succeed than a constant insistence that they must do the same as everyone else, which they never will.*

Perhaps the work will need to be done at a different time of day from school; evenings or even at weekends, though that would require changes to the registration regulations if schools are to be able to recognise it as attendance. The work could be as well as some time in more formal lessons or in some other provision as an alternative. It must be accredited and lead to proper qualifications. But perhaps a foreman or shift supervisor will be a more accessible role-model than a teacher. Perhaps parents will be more motivated to support their child if they can see some positive benefit from what they are doing all day. Maybe we even need to recognise that by age 14 or 15 some children, already living as virtual adults in the rest of their lives, have outgrown school entirely and it's just not the right place for them. Why not let them start apprenticeships or training courses that are normally available only at post-16? (There are signs that the government is now moving in this direction with new kinds of vocational schools, but that will still be too restrictive for some). Again the money would have to follow them but I can't see that they are any less ready for the world of work than their contemporaries were in the past. I am not advocating sending them back up chimneys, but work-based learning might just work where school has not.

Home education

I am now treading on very dangerous ground and many families who are a concern to us will not be appropriate for this alternative. But given the problems of those who are chronic non-attenders, is it ever an option? I think it might be, at least for a while, provided the parent is willing to accept some involvement by the LA. This is not about allowing 'flexi-schooling' for those parents who want it, but about whether flexibility might sometimes be the best way to keep vulnerable children engaged. We often end up with School Attendance Order proceedings when we know that the prospect of successful integration into a school at this time is pretty unlikely. If the child hasn't been receiving much formal education before, as an SAO requires, they will be way behind everyone else and this will be far too big a step all in one go, especially by secondary school age. Perhaps some kind of half-way arrangement that provides the parent with some support is more realistic at this point.

It would certainly help if the funding normally given to schools could be made available for such an approach. (It seems most unfair that LAs are sometimes criticised for not providing more help to home-educating parents when they haven't been funded to do so and parents don't have to tell them they're doing it!) But a few children might be classed as 'home educated', and therefore not included in schools' statistics, and perhaps specialist peripatetic teachers might be able to take responsibility for overseeing what they do with their parents. If this still enables the child to do some supervised work, without the daily arguments over school, it might at least enable the hole everyone is currently digging not to get any bigger. Parents do often have skills and aptitudes to share, if not always those that match what is offered in a school. Their own literacy and numeracy is obviously often an issue, so perhaps we should think more in terms of the whole family learning together.

If the parents are to remain in the driving seat, we will have to accept that what they provide might not look much like what happens in a school. But it doesn't have to – that's the whole point of home education. Take the travelling community, for example. Their children rarely go on to secondary education, though we have been rather more successful in keeping them in primary schools than used to be the case. I regret this lack of engagement – I'm sure the young people would benefit from at least some of the curriculum – but many don't want to be in a school. There are those who are showing signs that they do now want more formal education in order to broaden their career and lifestyle options. If so, they should be able to access it. But for most, learning the ways of their family and culture is much more important to them.

The only legal test of what home education should deliver is that the young person should be equipped for their adult life. On that definition, the travelling community can score quite well. I was once served with coffee by an impeccable and efficient PA in the immaculate caravan of a highly successful scrap metal dealer. This, of course, was the 15 year-old girl I had come to talk about and who kept all his accounts. It was impossible to suggest that she had not been 'properly educated' even though she hadn't been near a school for years. Perhaps we ought to be more relaxed about situations like this. We often don't have a better solution to offer anyway.

Like everything else, it is open to abuse but I think I am prepared to accept virtually any arrangement that ensures at least some education is involved. If 'flexi-schooling' is now acceptable, then a 'flexi-learning' approach strikes me as no different. That has to be more worthwhile than endless fruitless home visits or a notional prosecution that we all know won't change anything.

FREQUENTLY ASKED QUESTIONS ABOUT INTER-AGENCY WORKING

What's the difference between education 'welfare' and education 'social work'?

LAs historically chose which title to use, though few now employ only social workers to support schools rather than EWOs. However, some LAs are now placing social workers from their social care service into schools, so this may mean they become more common again! Others call their staff 'attendance officers', 'educational engagement officers' or 'attendance enforcement officers' etc. In general, I still prefer the word 'welfare' to be in there somewhere as it identifies the individual as concerned for the general welfare of children within the education system and not all families react well to the 'social worker' label. The work covers a whole variety of issues, not all of which are the natural province of social workers. However, EWOs (or their equivalent) should certainly use social work skills, including assessment, family conferencing, drawing up agreements and devising problem-solving action plans.

How is education welfare funded?

At present, schools, whatever their management status, cannot be charged for the LA's statutory work but this may mean that the provision is extremely limited. They may have to pay for additional support, either individually or through collective agreements made across local schools. This will usually fund a level of support according to a formula agreed with the LA, possibly at different levels of payment. These services will normally be targeted at those schools whose attendance is worst. New kinds of partnerships for behaviour and attendance are also becoming more common, especially involving secondary schools, which may involve the transfer of greater resources into school budgets or a more active role for headteachers in their day-to-day distribution and management.

Can schools fund EWOs themselves?

Increasing numbers of LAs have delegated at least part of the budget to schools for them to provide or buy back certain services. Most schools 'top up' their provision or employ additional support staff themselves to carry out some of the non-statutory work. (There is nothing to stop a school calling these people EWOs but school-employed workers do not have the legal authority and enforcement powers that LA officers have. This must be clear). It is important to remember that the LA is responsible for *all* the children in its area, including those in the private sector and those who are home educated, out of school, excluded or missing, not just those children who are registered pupils at state schools.

Is enforcing attendance the main job of an LA officer?

It is very important but they will often also have duties under child protection and safeguarding procedures and may help to administer entitlement to free school meals or other discretionary benefits. They may be involved in the regulation of children in part-time work and a range of other functions to promote the welfare of children in education, which may vary between different areas. Some EWOs (or their equivalent) organise holiday clubs for disadvantaged children, work with children with special needs and with those who are either excluded or at risk of it. Many will offer specialist advice and information to schools and parents about 'parental responsibility' under the Children Act 1989 and other key pastoral issues. They may advise on bullying or drug abuse and help to resolve the frequent disputes which arise between parents and schools over issues like discipline, uniform, homework etc.

Do we have to take part in arrangements under the Common Assessment Framework?

It will depend on local protocols but the general answer has to be 'yes'. School is such an important part of a child's life and what goes on there is so vital for their current and future wellbeing that it is hard to conceive of an effective inter-agency strategy that left the school out. Some of these arrangements may have to be dovetailed with the new arrangements for multi-agency responses to children with SEN once they are introduced as, on the face of it, the procedures look very similar and will often involve the same families.

Can a child go into 'care' for not attending school?

Not on these grounds specifically (as used to be the case before the Children Act 1989). Children can only be removed from their parents' care on grounds of 'significant harm'. But non-attendance could be a risk factor, alongside others in some cases. It may be agreed with the parents that a child or young person is 'accommodated' voluntarily where family problems have become acute. These could include not attending school.

Is not sending your child to school 'neglect'?

Unlike failing to ensure that your child attends medical appointments, it is not specifically mentioned in the definitions, (see '*Working Together to Safeguard Children*' 2013). But there is no doubt that prolonged absence can have a harmful effect on a child's 'social and intellectual development' – part of the definition of 'significant harm' in the Children Act 1989. It may not be realistic to expect intervention by social care on these grounds alone, but if non-attendance is part of a bigger picture, as it often is, it should certainly be addressed as part of the assessment. If a child is placed on a child protection plan, ensuring school attendance should certainly be included as part of the action the parent is required to take, whatever the reason the plan was originally needed.

Why don't LAs always prosecute when I want them to?

Mainly because it isn't always the solution. The procedure will take up a considerable amount of time and there has to be sufficient evidence. Schools must be prepared to leave absences unauthorised and this is not always possible. There should be clear agreement in each area about the criteria for bringing a prosecution and what procedures need to be followed first. Decision-making should be according to a set timetable so that suitable cases for prosecution are identified and action taken at the appropriate time. However, many situations of chronic poor attendance will not be resolved by action through the Courts and resources are unlikely to allow more cases to proceed than have some realistic chance of being improved as a result.

Can headteachers take legal action or issue Penalty Notices themselves?

No. Only the LA currently has the necessary powers. This was proposed, at least for academies, in Charlie Taylor's 2012 Report but it has not happened and I am not convinced that many headteachers would actually want it. Many legal issues might be raised which could become very costly. The procedures are becoming increasingly complex and even routine cases are sometimes contested by solicitors. Headteachers have to provide the evidence in the form of a copy of the register and, if necessary, a written 's.9 statement'. The power does exist for headteachers to issue Penalty Notices on the LA's behalf but this can *only* be done under an agreed Code of Conduct with the LA which defines the criteria as they have to prosecute if the parent does not pay. They are the LA's Penalty Notices, (and they still get the money even if the school issues them!) so they will usually want to control the process in order to ensure that mistakes are not made that could later be challenged.

How are services for children inspected?

Through a unified LA-level Ofsted Children's Services inspection alongside social workers and others. Individual school inspections may also include comment on the external services that are available to support the school.

Do teachers and LA officers have the right to go into people's houses to look for truants?

Only by invitation. They have no right of forced entry under any circumstances – only the Police can do that. In general, most children's workers will prefer not to be alone with a child without a parent present for reasons of safeguarding, though practice varies. EWOs may be a little more relaxed about this than social workers. With all the concerns about the risks to both professionals and children, most agencies are having to re-think their procedures and to ensure that expectations about what they are able to do are reasonable. Officers will increasingly be trying to visit only by appointment with parents or to meet them in neutral venues, rather than simply knocking on the door when they are not expected, even if this makes it more difficult to catch children at home unexpectedly.

Can anyone physically make a child come to school?

No. Even under an Education Supervision Order a supervisor can only 'advise, assist and befriend' and give 'directions'. All other relationships with children are entirely voluntary. Even children in care have to be encouraged, not forced. The days have long gone when officers could be expected to bring a child into school if they will not co-operate. Even the Police will have problems returning a child to school who is actively resisting. This confrontational approach is totally unreasonable and counter-productive – the school could not itself detain a child against their will, even once they had been brought in kicking and screaming! Other skills like persuasion, patience and persistence are required, as in all work with children.

We have a counselling service provided by the school nurse who sees children who have had frequent absences for illness. Can I require her to tell me what a child has said to them?

Probably not, though it would be helpful they could at least suggest strategies that might have a chance of success. But school nurses and other health workers may have a higher standard of confidentiality than many teachers are used to. This could include information about the young person's sexual activity or medical needs, though if these affect the way they need to be managed in school, it is best if information can be shared, though this will normally depend on the child's consent. They might not want staff at the school to know this much about them. However, the worker must share any child protection information, but not necessarily with the school.

Can we check the reasons given for a child's absence with their doctor?

Only with the parents' consent. They, or another member of the surgery team, may be willing to give a general view on whether the child is fit for school without revealing precise medical information.

CHAPTER 6

NARRATIVE CASE-STUDIES

These stories are intended to illustrate the complexity of many casework situations and to explore how the various legal powers available might best be used to bring about an effective outcome for the child. Even if all else seems to have failed and action has to be taken on a statutory basis, the law still has to be applied with pastoral sensitivity if there is to be any real hope of bringing about genuine change. It will indeed be a tragic day for our most vulnerable children if there is no longer anyone available to demonstrate this kind of perseverance and commitment.

JOEL
Referral

Joel (aged 9) lives with his family in a well-established community of travellers. They have several resting places and, when he is at one of these, Joel is usually admitted to the local school for a few weeks at a time before moving on. His mother has always been keen for him to go to school before, but it is now four months since he went in and no-one is too sure whether he is still on a register anywhere. Following concerns raised by members of the local community, the case is referred to the LA for an initial assessment.

Initial response

Angela, the EWO for the area where the community is now staying, has a number of investigative tasks to do:

- She visits the site in partnership with the field officers from the local Traveller Education Service. Joel's mother is ambiguous about whether he is there. She says he is, but he is currently visiting his grandma in the south of England. He may be back next week. Angela leaves a form for a parent to complete about whether they intend to educate Joel themselves with support from the Travellers' tutor or whether they want to admit him to the local school, as they expect to be on the present site for the winter.

- The last school Joel attended is contacted to see if he is still on their registers. They report that they took him off their admission register after four weeks continuous absence as neither they nor their EWO knew where the family had gone. Angela asks for his (very limited) educational records to be sent to the LA. The headteacher mentions that Joel has some learning difficulties and is still at the very early stages of independent reading, but this may only be because he has missed much of the work.

- Angela contacts the local primary school about admitting Joel. The headteacher is initially reluctant, feeling he may not stay long. Angela advises that Joel is entitled to a place as the school is not full in the relevant year group, if that is what the parents request. The headteacher is especially concerned about Joel's possible learning difficulties as her special needs budget is already overspent!

Practice point: *As Joel is no longer on a school register he is not 'absent' and his parents cannot be said to be committing any offence. However, his current educational status is unclear as he is neither a registered pupil nor identified as being educated 'otherwise'. The first priority will be to resolve this issue. There is also the key question of Joel's special needs and the implications this may have for the provision he requires, but there is no evidence that a mainstream school is inappropriate. The Admissions Code of Practice does not allow admissions authorities (or headteachers) to refuse or delay admission on the grounds of a child's past history or potential special needs.*

Early stages

No reply is received from Joel's parents about how they intend to educate him so Angela visits the following week with the Stage 1 letter for a possible School Attendance Order. There is some concern that the moment things become official, the family will simply move on again. She wants to give them every opportunity to make other arrangements if that is what they wish to do. On arrival at the site a boy who she takes to be Joel runs off as she knocks on the caravan door. Joel's mum confirms that he is back and that she would like him to go to the local school. No formal letters are left and Angela arranges to take Joel and his mum to the school later in the week.

After a false start when Joel and his mum weren't at home, a meeting is held on the Friday afternoon. Angela tries to build on Joel's mum's willingness to address his needs and especially the fact that he is significantly behind in his reading. Joel's mum agrees that this will be a considerable problem to him in future and, as she is a very limited reader herself, she does not want him to have the same problems. It is agreed that Joel will be admitted from the following Monday and Joel's mum is helped to compete the necessary forms. Joel's mum seems pleased with the decision and promises to get his uniform sorted out over the weekend.

> **Practice point:** *The key issue now becomes the fact that Joel must become a 'registered pupil'. It has been agreed that the 'otherwise' option is inappropriate. Joel must now be placed on the admission register from the agreed date, whether or not he actually arrives.*

Monday morning

The headteacher rings Angela at 9.30 to say that Joel has not turned up as expected. Angela confirms that he will still be admitted and marked as unauthorised absent and makes a visit to the site later in the day. Joel's father is at home alone. He says that he only came back from working away at the weekend and knows nothing about Joel going to school. His wife and Joel have gone away 'for a few days'. Angela again explains the need for Joel to receive education, and his reading difficulty. She also explains that Joel has now been registered at the school and will be unauthorised absent from now on if he does not go without good reason. This is an offence by the parents. On getting back to the office, Angela advises the headteacher of the situation and that the school must leave his absences unauthorised for the time being.

The education records have arrived from the previous school. There is also a confidential section about a child protection concern that was referred six months ago when Joel came to the school with redenning to his buttocks. There is no indication of what the outcome was. Angela contacts the local social work service and asks them to check with the previous LA whether the child protection issue was resolved and whether Joel was the subject of a child protection plan. Some concern is raised that Joel has not been seen since his dad came home.

Practice point: *Schools are entitled to keep confidential data about child protection issues which do not have to be disclosed to parents. As far as possible this information should be passed in confidence to the designated teacher in the receiving school or the designated officer in the receiving local authority education service. Obviously this cannot be done if you do not know where the child has gone. In this case, make sure the child's basic details are posted on the Missing Pupils section of the School2School database and keep the records in case they are needed in future.*

The following weeks

Joel still doesn't arrive at the school and no reply is received from his parents. There are now three weeks' continuous unauthorised absence, enough for a Penalty Notice to be considered. Angela makes another visit with the Travelling Service and this time Joel is at home with his mum, safe and well. Again she agrees to admit Joel to the school and Angela agrees to collect them both the following morning. This time all goes well. Joel is ready, if not yet with all his uniform and seems quite happy to stay at the school when they leave him. The social worker has now traced the child protection records. The previous incident was confirmed as over-chastisement and Joel's dad was cautioned by the Police. Joel was not case-conferenced and the school are advised to report any further concerns immediately.

Progress

Angela gets regular calls from Joel's school over the next few weeks. His attendance is about 70% since he started. Most of the absence is not covered by any notes but he seems happy and settled when he is there. She confirms with the school that this absence has all been left unauthorised as before, though the headteacher is not very happy at the impact on her figures! Joel has been assessed for his special needs and they are trying to address his problems, though this is made more difficult by his erratic attendance. There have been no child protection concerns raised and, when he comes, he is always on time and well looked-after.

Angela makes occasional visits to the family and it is agreed that a meeting will be held to review the Contract. At the meeting, the headteacher suggests that Joel's mum comes into the school a couple of times a week to help him (and herself) with reading. She seems very keen on this idea.

Practice point: *Joel is a 'child in need' under the Children Act 1989 (s.17) by virtue of his poor school attendance, his special needs and the past history of concern about his safety. This entitles him and his family to services, which may be arranged through use of the Common Assessment Framework if a multi-agency response is required, but much depends on whether families are willing to ask for support. The threshold of 'significant harm', or the risk of it, has to be met before anything could happen against their wishes.*

Crisis!

A few weeks later the school rings to say that Joel's mum has been in and told them he won't be coming again. Angela asks the school to keep him on their registers while the situation is clarified. She visits the site and Joel is there with his mum. She says that his dad has changed his mind about the school and he won't send him any more. Angela advises her that this might result in prosecution but is keen to avoid this if at all possible because it will just reinforce their alienation from the system. It is agreed that Joel will come off the registers again and be supported by the Travellers' tutor for the time being as educated 'otherwise'. Mum will need a lot of support in managing the work between visits but perhaps it will help her skills as well to do the work with Joel.

> **Practice point:** *Joel would have to be left on the registers and his absences left unauthorised if there is to be any evidence that could be used against his parents. Once he is no longer 'absent' and not registered at any school, only a School Attendance Order is possible. This is rather more complicated than prosecution but parents do have the right to educate their children in other ways if they want to.*

Conclusion

It might seem that the LA was being over-tolerant of Joel's limited engagement with education, but a Penalty Notice or prosecution is very unlikely to change the situation, assuming the parents stayed to answer the summons. They might well pay a fine, but would this necessarily get Joel back into school? On the other hand, Joel is entitled to an education and has a right to develop to his full potential. By agreeing to try and support Joel in being educated through a tuition support service, at least for the time being, Angela is hoping that this will keep him sufficiently motivated for his family to think again about school in the future. Only time will tell.

ALLEN

Referral

Allen (aged 12) lives with his mum and 2 younger sisters and spends every other weekend with his dad following his parents' divorce three years ago. The whole family are irregular attenders at their schools, usually managing only 4 days most weeks. Mondays or Fridays are regularly missed. Allen`s mum nearly always sends a note in with him when he returns. These say things like he had a cold or his mum needed him to help with the other children. The family aren`t on the phone and the mobile number they have given is now inactive. Staff at the school often don't get an answer when letters are sent home and Allen`s mum has missed two or three meetings arranged at the school to discuss his absences, all of which have so far been authorised by the school because of the notes. School staff are aware that Allen`s dad recently did a month in prison for not paying a fine and his mum is on benefits so any future fine is not likely to be very substantial.

Initial response

Colin, the school's EWO has known Allen's family for several years and colleagues even remember when his mum was a poor attender herself. She had Allen when she was only 16 and, in fact, her ex-husband, the father of the other two children is not Allen's actual father, to whom his mum was never married. Allen is not aware of this and has had no contact with his real dad at all.

> **Practice point:** *The definitions of the Children Act 1989 can be very important in determining which 'parents' schools/LAs have to work with and their respective legal status. Although the man Allen calls 'dad' does not actually have any legal relationship to him, (though he has 'parental responsibility' for his half-sisters on exactly the same basis as Allen's mum), this will probably not be an issue unless she objects to his involvement. Should Allen and his 'dad' ever live*

> *together, it might be wise to consider a s.8 residence order which would give him a legal status, especially if Allen's mum does not support the arrangement. The court could then decide what was best for Allen at the time.*

Colin knows that there is little chance of bringing about a dramatic change in this family under current circumstances. He visits Allen's mum and tries to explain that the situation is serious. Allen should be in school full time and he's never really settled. Allen's mum consistently says that she sends him in every time he is well enough but he has a lot of chest infections (the house is rather damp and cold in winter) and it takes him a long time to get over them. Colin arranges to collect her and bring her into school for a meeting with the head.

Meeting at school

This meeting has a number of important issues to address:

- can more be done to stop Allen having so much absence through illness?

- is this the real reason?

- should the school continue authorising the absences just on the basis of a note from his mum?

- does she appreciate how much time he has had away from school?

- could Allen's 'dad' have a more active role to play in improving the situation?

- is there anything in school which is making Allen reluctant to attend?

- is there anything outside school which is influencing him?

The school prepares a computerised printout of Allen's attendance record in advance of the meeting and Colin (who is chairing the meeting rather than the head to make his mum feel more at ease), goes through it with her. Allen and his mum both admit they hadn't realised he was having so many days away and that he had missed so many Mondays and Fridays. A new explanation emerges at the meeting. Some of the absences are because he can't always get back from visiting his dad on a Sunday and Allen has to wait for a friend of his dad's to bring him home on a Monday morning. By then he reckons it's not worth going into school 'as he only has PE in the afternoon'.

> **Practice point:** *The issue of children's visits to parents overlapping with school time is becoming more common; including having supervised contact where there are complications like a history of violence or abuse, or children visiting parents in prison. Where parents tell the truth about these arrangements, (though some may not), they could be authorised as 'exceptional circumstances' provided they do not happen too often. It may be necessary for the school to make representations to the parent, social worker or probation officer if the visits are disrupting the child's education beyond the occasional day. The kinds of problems presented in Allen's case would not normally justify absences being authorised, except in an unavoidable emergency.*

Parenting Contract

It is agreed with Allen's mum that there must now be some kind of Contract drawn up about what she must do if he is genuinely unable to come to school. Allen will be taken to the doctor if he is not fit for school beyond one day and Colin is given written permission to check with the doctor whether he has been seen each time. The school will not authorise the absence beyond one day unless he has been taken to the doctor. Colin explains the consequences of leaving the absences unauthorised and that this could be evidence that can be used for a Penalty Notice. No absences will be authorised just because Allen is late back from his dad's; he must come in on Mondays, even if he is late. The school has an active parents group and Allen's mum is told she is expected to come to it on Wednesday afternoons. It's an opportunity to talk about the problems of bringing up children and for her to get some support from other mums.

Colin asks permission from Allen and his mum to contact his 'dad' and try to get him to take a greater interest in Allen's education. The head, who did not previously have any details about him, agrees to write and invite him into school and to make sure he is invited to the next parent's evening. Allen's mum is skeptical but Allen seems rather pleased about this. As the meeting is ending, Allen says he doesn't have any PE kit and the school agree to get him some, provided he attends full time for the next three weeks. The head promises to explain to the PE teacher that Allen will have to wear whatever he can find next week.

Practice point: *Parenting Contracts are entirely voluntary, but they can be helpful in defining objectives and setting timescales. They are not the same as home school agreements which may define the basis of the child's admission, though, these too are not compulsory and cannot then be used as the grounds for removing a child from the school once admitted if the school judges that the agreement has failed. Parenting Contracts are intended to provide the parents with something extra to help them, not just define what they must do. Their refusal or failure, however, could be cited later if the LA takes statutory enforcement action later.*

The next six weeks

The Contract is signed by everyone and circulated and things are quiet for the rest of the week. Colin writes to Allen's 'dad'. Things go well on the first Monday; the PE teacher provides the kit and Allen plays five-a-side, which he didn't know they were doing. He is absent on the Friday, but comes in on the Monday with a note saying he 'really did have a cold'! When his dad gets in touch with Colin it is obvious that he doesn't really want to get too involved. He has another family of his own now and, although he didn't mind looking after Allen when they were all together, he would now like to ease Allen away from his regular visits. After all the problems he has had with debts he is thinking of moving further away with his new family to make a fresh start. Now that he knows about all the absences, (the school had sent him a copy of the register), he thinks it's best if Allen doesn't come to stay any more weekends. It's time Allen knew that he is not actually his dad. Colin says he would like to talk this through as he thinks Allen will be very disappointed, but his dad puts the phone down and there is no further contact from him.

Crisis!

The following Monday afternoon Colin gets a phone call from Allen's mum who has gone round to a neighbour's house in a panic. She says Allen has been expelled! Colin gets in touch with the school and establishes that Allen has been excluded for three days for swearing at a teacher. At the home visit Allen explains that he was upset because his 'dad' has told him the truth and that he won't be able to stay with him any more. Colin helps Allen to write a letter to the teacher apologising for his swearing. But this incident, coupled with the rejection, has unsettled Allen and his attendance begins to become very erratic. He starts going into town when his mum thinks he's at school, or refusing to get out of bed so that she has to leave him behind when she takes the little ones. She's managed to get a job in the mornings but this means she doesn't have the time to spend at home trying to get him to go. Neither has she been going to the parent's group. Once or twice Colin calls round when Allen is absent and finds him at home with another lad from his year group. His unauthorised absences are now over 30%. A meeting is held to review the Contract which has clearly failed, but Allen won't come.

> **Practice point:** *Although Allen's attendance has deteriorated, it is difficult to see whether the use of legal powers would be useful. 'Truancy' is not a crime and Allen himself is making all the decisions now, not his mum. He is angry, disappointed and disaffected. Fining his mum will not change that – but it may have to be done anyway just to make the point and to try and change Allen's behaviour before he gets too alienated from school. Allen's behaviour is not putting him at enough risk to warrant compulsory intervention under the Children Act 1989 – he's just lost all faith in school and probably in all the adults who have been trying to help him.*

Conclusion

Allen makes an erratic start to his next year in secondary school and in the end the LA, after a formal warning, rather reluctantly serves a Penalty Notice on his mum. She doesn't pay and is subsequently fined £75 to be paid at £3 a week. Colin explains to Allen that things will only get worse for his mum if he doesn't get to school more often. Things do gradually improve, partly because his mum now has a new boyfriend who takes a real interest in Allen. They go fishing at weekends with his own son and he makes it clear that Allen must go to school. Colin and the school are trying to build a new relationship with him as he now seems to be the key 'parental' figure in Allen's life. There are some real signs of encouragement but there's still a long way to go!

FREYDA

Referral

Freyda (aged 7) has Downs Syndrome and is a statemented pupil at a special unit in a mainstream school for children with moderate learning difficulties. She is supposed to come to school by taxi but is often not ready when it calls. Her mum sometimes rings to say that she overslept; sometimes she is away for a few days without explanation. Freyda also has a considerable amount of time off through sickness and there is some concern that her parents don't always seem to think it's worth taking her to the doctor. Freyda needs regular speech therapy but is often not at school to receive it or isn't brought for clinic appointments. The school has had difficulty contacting her parents but they always seem well-meaning. Other professionals who have been involved with the family feel that her parents have learning difficulties themselves and do not really understand Freyda's needs.

Initial response

Comfort, the EWO for the area in which Freyda lives does not know the family as there are no other children. The unit has its own welfare assistant, but as Freyda lives 6 miles away it is difficult to maintain regular contact. Comfort goes and talks the case over with her before making a home visit in the evening when both parents and Freyda are at home. The house is in a poor state and very short of furniture. Freyda is watching TV and eating chips from the shop. She is reluctant to talk to Comfort. Her dad seems to have been drinking and her mum is very quiet. They say that they can't really see what all the fuss is about; Freyda goes to school as often as possible, but they don't feel there is much point as she is 'never going to learn anything'. It turns out that her dad had an older sister with Downs Syndrome who is in a 'home' and they expect the same to happen to Freyda in the long run.

Comfort explains that times have changed and that there is no reason why Freyda cannot benefit from education and learn the skills she needs to live more independently when she grows up. Her parents promise to try and make sure she goes more regularly. Comfort offers to take them and Freyda to the next speech therapy appointment herself and encourages them to make contact with a local support group for parents whose children have a learning disability.

> **Practice point:** *Children with identified special educational needs can raise particular issues about the legal requirements for attendance. Their parents must ensure that they are educated in accordance with their 'age, ability and aptitude, and any special educational needs they may have'. This is not just about sending them to school as there will be a variety of wider issues to be addressed if the child is to benefit from the education provided. In a sense, parents of such children have a greater obligation than others and more than just attendance may be relevant in determining whether they have fulfilled it.*

Assessment of Freyda's needs

It is clear that there are a variety of wider issues beyond simply seeing this as an attendance problem. Comfort suggests bringing forward Freyda's annual statement review and a meeting is arranged at school involving the key professionals. She brings Freyda's mum to the meeting, but her dad is at work. At the meeting it is agreed to renew the attempts at speech therapy and to provide Freyda's parents with a new assessment of her skills and capabilities. She is doing well in school but there are signs that it is only in school that she shows any of these skills; at home she just sits in front of the TV and is much less communicative. Freyda's mum says that she sometimes has to smack her because she is 'very stubborn and will not do as she is told'. The staff try to help her to see that this may be because she is frustrated and bored and that greater stimulation and activity in her life will help her. They suggest a programme that involves activities sent home by the school and something each weekend to get her out of the house and meeting other children. Freyda's mum seems to have little idea of what her interests are and what she may be capable of doing with a bit of encouragement. Comfort agrees to keep in regular contact for a while and to bring Freyda's parents to the school once every half term to see her work and meet her teachers.

Child protection referral

A few Mondays later, Comfort is notified of a child protection referral over the weekend. The police were called to Freyda's house late on Saturday night. Her dad had been drinking and had got into a violent fight with her mum. When they got there, Freyda was outside in the street crying and being comforted by a neighbour. The neighbour alleged to the police that her dad had been 'messing with her'. Social workers were immediately informed and when they visited, it was agreed that Freyda be accommodated with a specialist foster family while the matter was investigated.

> **Practice point:** *The police should always check whether there are child protection issues behind an incident of domestic violence, as this is a frequent risk indicator of both emotional and physical abuse. They have the power to remove a child into police protection if they are in immediate danger. Only the police can remove a child in this way without a court order. It is often better if the alleged abuser can be encouraged to leave the home rather than the child, though, as in this case, the child's needs may be such that being looked after may be in their best interests, at least for a short time. No statutory powers have been used; Freyda's parents are free to remove her at any time.*

The child protection investigation is inconclusive. Freyda's dad denies all allegations and the evidence from the neighbour is very vague, based primarily on things Freyda has said to her. Under DVD interview Freyda is frightened and confused and makes no obvious allegation herself that could be used as evidence. Her mum agrees to her having a medical examination but this too provides nothing of significance. There is some concern that Freyda's parents will simply leave her in the foster family. Her dad has already said he doesn't want her home again because of the allegations. The case conference feels that Freyda should be the subject of a child protection plan if she goes home.

As well as the allegation about possible sexual abuse, there is also the report from Comfort that her mum smacks her when she won't do as she's told. There have also been some examples of injuries reported by staff at the school in the past that Comfort was not previously aware of. There is general concern about the standard of care and lack of awareness of Freyda's needs. While in foster care, her school attendance is 100% but it is a short-term provision and she cannot stay there. There is some suggestion by the health workers that a residential placement with education on the premises may be best for her but this would need joint funding. In the end, Freyda's mum says she wants her home. It is arranged that she spends one weekend a month and some school holidays in respite care which she really enjoys. Her attendance is generally acceptable and there are no further concerns in the short term although things are still a bit rough and ready. Her dad keeps a very low profile and there are suggestions that he is now living somewhere else much of the time. The school provides a member of the core group which monitors Freyda on a daily basis.

> **Practice point:** *A child protection plan places schools under an obligation to make sure that the child is safe on a daily basis. There need to be special procedures in place for information about any absences to be passed to the child's keyworker. The general thrust of the Children Act 1989 is that children should be looked after by their own families as far as possible, though not if this threatens their welfare. This can be a higher risk strategy rather than removing children but the threshold for deciding that parents are not fit to look after their own children is rightly high.*

Longer term issues

After six months, the child protection plan comes to an end as no further incidents or concerns have been raised. Inevitably many of the agencies pull out at this point, the short-stay places are reduced, and Freyda's school attendance begins to deteriorate again. Her mum is now on her own with Freyda and, although she sometimes manages to do things with her, Freyda still spends far too much time on her own watching TV. Comfort is still very concerned about Freyda and a formal process of consultation with other professionals is held. Legal advisors still feel that there are insufficient grounds for statutory action and that poor attendance at school is now the only major presenting problem. After trying to convince Freyda's mum that she must get her to school more regularly, it is decided to seek an Education Supervision Order under the Children Act 1989 to try and introduce a greater degree of structure and authority into the situation.

> **Practice point:** *Education officers must consult social care before seeking an ESO in order to be sure that some other action, outside their own power, is not more appropriate. The court must be satisfied that the child not being properly educated and that the order is 'better for the child than no order', having regard to the child's needs, especially their education. They apply the 'welfare checklist' before making any order; it is not simply an automatic process. Once the order is made, the parent is committing an offence if they do not follow the Supervisor's 'directions' and, should the child not co-operate, social workers must make a full assessment of the situation if asked to do so.*

Education Supervision Order

The Court agrees that the application is in Freyda's best interests and makes an order lasting one year. The Action Plan sets out what everyone will to do to address Freyda's educational, health and social care needs. Comfort is allocated as the Supervisor, with support from a colleague and welfare staff at the school who form a kind of 'core group' to review progress on a regular basis. Freyda's mum co-operates fully and even begins to enjoy the attention. She starts to see Comfort as a friend and, at times, Comfort is worried that she is becoming too dependent on her. Freyda's school attendance is now excellent and, bearing in mind the deterioration once the agencies pulled out before, and Freyda's long term special needs, it is agreed to apply to have the order extended for another two years. Comfort also involves the local parents network and makes a direction under the order that Freyda's mum must attend their meetings.

Conclusion

Comfort is aware that she cannot go on giving this amount of support for the rest of Freyda's education, (which should continue at least until she is 19). It may well be best for some kind of residential placement to be identified. This is a key question to be considered at the next review of Freyda's statement. Whether it can be done will depend on whether her priority is high enough and sufficient resources are available. Otherwise, her attendance is likely to require constant monitoring and continuing interventions.

CONCLUSION

So where are we in our thinking about attendance and absence from school? Even while this book has been undergoing preparation for publication, there have been yet more changes. Holidays have become another kind of 'truancy' and many perfectly law-abiding parents are now finding themselves criticised and at risk of being fined because they choose to take a short break with their children in term-time, (or feel they have no choice). Nothing seems to have come from the on-line petition, but there is still pressure for a more realistic approach, which I personally would welcome. Some schools do seem to have slightly over-reacted; they have not been told they can *never* agree to it, though that's what they have decided to do. 'Leave' is still permitted in 'exceptional' circumstances and I can think of plenty. I don't doubt that the government won't change the general principle, but I think it is becoming increasingly clear that 11 million children and their parents can't all take their summer holiday in the same 6 weeks. That simply doesn't fit with the reality of people's working lives and the travel and leisure industry would virtually disappear without the year-round business. The problem of children who have changed schools since their holiday was booked is one particularly thorny issue. How can you get permission in advance from a school your child doesn't go to? There are also real questions about what families with cultural links overseas are supposed to do when their family events do not fit with school terms built around the Christian calendar, as well as the issues raised by different schools with different holiday periods where parents have children in each of them!

Schools will have their whole-year data published for the first time in 2014 and we await what the impact of that will be. I suspect it will show a small increase in overall absence. Fewer children are having a lot of time off, which is particularly welcome, if the figures are to be trusted, though there may well be more absence in total once the 6th half-term is included. It is not entirely clear whether 'persistent absence' will also cover the whole year and what the government will do with the data it has collected on the attendance of 4 year-olds. These changes will make year-on-year comparisons difficult as the counting periods will be different. I hope no-one will make judgments on trends without being careful to check that like is being compared with like. We have also had the extension of the 'participation' age, with more to follow, but again, it must be made clear that this is not an extension of 'compulsory school age' and sixth form data must be excluded. I have already seen talk in the media of 'truanting' sixth formers and of 'compulsory' education now going beyond Year 11.

Having said all that, I really don't want to say any more about the data. That is one of our fundamental problems about school attendance. It's *all* about the data now that we have so much of it; except, of course, that it isn't. In the old days I used to go into a school to look at their paper registers in order to identify those children who weren't there, not to check the sums! It often took some time, especially as not everyone was as diligent in marking their registers as they should have been, but that was clearly understood as the reason why I was there. No-one was too much bothered about the pages at the back with the totals on. But once it was all done electronically and levels of the various kinds of absence became part of the process of making public judgments about schools, the whole game changed.

Why do we have all these data-collection arrangements in place? Why do schools keep registers at all? The fundamental reason is to ensure that children receive an appropriate education. But we have turned it into an audit process about *schools* which has now become the priority. Most headteachers, governors, LAs and politicians now regard attendance and absence as a school management issue and so making the figures look as good as possible has become the overwhelming objective. Children who might undermine that primary aim have become a liability to be avoided if at all possible and finding ways of improving the data has taken over from making sure that they actually come to school. As long as we can find a way to record the session as something other than unauthorised absence, and ideally as an attendance, then everyone is happy. My former colleagues in LAs now spend as much time looking at computers as they do talking to schools, children and families. That can't be right.

Anecdotally, I can evidence this from the regular training sessions that I run as well as from my wider experience. We spend more time talking about what code to put in the registers than on anything else. If I don't include it I have to find time to put it in. Everyone is worried that their school will be compared unfavourably with other schools, (and most claim that they are the only one in their area doing it properly!) 'Can we find a way of recording this given situation in a way that won't reflect badly on our performance?' has become the most pressing enquiry. I would rather be talking about 'What could we be doing to help this child get back into education?' but somehow it never seems to be quite as important. For all the time and effort we spend on getting the data right, I am not convinced that it tells us anything at all about children or their parents. It is seen as much more about evaluating schools, not for ensuring that the genuine attendance of children is at the centre of all we do. In my view the data gives us very poor information about both requirements, because schools naturally want to present themselves in as favourable a light as possible. I don't blame them. We may be able to make a judgment from the figures about how efficient the school is in its procedures. We may even be able to admire their creativity. But as a meaningful tool for telling us anything about what is happening to real children's attendance and what needs to be done about it – well, draw your own conclusions!

So what *does* really matter? Despite the current government's reversal in language it is still, of course, every child. The priority, and given the current legal requirements perhaps this isn't always reflected as prominently as it should have been in the preceding pages, should be that it is children and young people themselves who need to engage more in their own learning if we are make any significant difference.

With younger children the emphasis rightly has to be on parents who make most of the key decisions for this age group. But many of those who come to the attention of LAs as adults had such bad educational experiences when *they* were at school that they now have an ambivalent attitude towards what is offered to their children. We are really still dealing with their own childhood educational deficit even if the trigger has been their role as a parent. I cannot count how many times I have sat in a Magistrates Court and felt that the unmet educational and other needs of the parent were clearly the basis of why we were all there 15 or 20 years later.

But the older children get, the more they will determine for themselves whether school is a place they want to be. Action against their parents seems increasingly irrelevant and does not, in fact, solve their problems and get them back in most cases. School surveys, both in connection with inspections of schools and LAs, and using specific tools such as 'Voice of the Learner' or 'Tellus', have enabled us to hear at first hand that most children enjoy school and come reasonably willingly, if only to be with their friends. Those from supportive families who understand that this is a crucial path to success in life will never trouble the absence scorers beyond the odd blip and the occasional week in the sun. We really do not need to worry about them, or their parents even if they are not there every possible day. Indeed doing so may distract us from what really needs to be done.

I regularly used to go into schools to present attendance prizes to halls full of smiling children and proud parents. Some manage 100% attendance over a whole year; a few attend 100% over as many as 5 consecutive years. We don't talk about that anything like enough or give those children and parents the credit they so richly deserve. School councils have given children a voice and the surveys also tell us that schools are increasingly listening to what they say about bullying or other issues that need to be addressed to make the school experience more enriching. Some schools have made real progress in improving attendance; not just as a statistical measure but in terms of genuinely improved participation. It's certainly not all doom and gloom or a waste of time trying. Much can be done and most of the time it works.

But I keep coming back to the 2-5% who are virtually nowhere to be seen. They were not there on the day the survey was completed. Their parents were not at the assembly and they will not become more positive at either the threat or the reality of fines and courts. The young people themselves, who undoubtedly have a wide range of skills and knowledge, (even if they are not those prescribed by the National Curriculum), are confident in their ability to get by. Many will do so, at least to their own satisfaction, and expecting them to remain engaged in formal learning until they are 18 or beyond, will be treated with equal derision. I'm afraid they do not believe that we have anything to teach them that they need to know. Or, at the very least, our generally institutional ways of learning that work for most will simply never work for them, even if some will find new ways to achieve through new opportunities presented through further education and other kinds of training. Not all is necessarily lost if we haven't got there by 16.

We cannot hope to solve every problem or reverse every negative influence unless these children and their families become more central to our thinking. I only ever hear politicians, and sadly many headteachers, talk about those who are 'hard-working'. Our educational policies are aimed at those families who 'want to get on' or are designed to let 'the cream rise to the top'. It may not always feel like this, but recent governments in particular seem keen to see schools primarily as places for challenging dissident values in the community as a whole that do not easily fit with these aspirations. This is seen by some families as professionals from another world trying to dictate how they should live; from the length of their children's hair to what time they should go to bed and what they get up to at the weekends. The teacher becomes a kind of angry parent figure who is constantly disappointed in you and critical of anything that contradicts what they say is right. They know they are not the kind of family the school really wants to attract and that society does not offer them much hope for the future. They have their own agenda, often very different from that of mainstream society. What is on offer, right down to the content of the curriculum, seems irrelevant. When school is all about the attainment of academic knowledge, passing exams, being successful and going to University and you know that your life isn't about any of those things, what hope is there for you? And if the school does try to be flexible and accommodate your needs, it is likely to then find itself judged as 'failing' so why should anyone bother?

But is this the way to bring out the best in *all* our children? This generally paternalistic approach is not how we expect to be treated by doctors, social workers and other professionals, who should take our own views much more into account than used to be the case. In general, we no longer expect to be told what to do with our own lives, or at least to be consulted and have our wishes and feelings taken into account, even if they can't always be followed. That approach to children and families is at the heart of the Children Act 1989, but when it comes to schools, the rules are often different. We live in an increasingly culturally and socially diverse society, but schools are expected to have a clear 'ethos'. They have to define themselves by certain values to maintain their identity, though in practice most of them are pretty much the same. This can seem exclusive to some families and stop them feeling that they belong anywhere. Not every parent necessarily shares those values or sees school as the most important defining factor in their life. As a result, their children feel lost there and may opt not to go as the easiest way to resolve the tension.

This is not just about individuals struggling to find their place in large rather impersonal settings, though that is certainly an important factor in understanding why some children stay away. It's more a question of the *dissonance* between two ways of life. School may be the thing that has to give way if the conflict becomes too much. Even children experiencing abuse feel that family nearly always comes first, even if that family is beset with problems or worse. Whatever our misgivings, if we are to have any hope of keeping these children on board we may have to meet them and their parents much more than half way. Lines in the sand do not help them to move forward. Some parents are intimidated by any contact with their children's teachers and react with hostility as a defence mechanism, just as they did when they went to school themselves. In particular, a given style and standard of behaviour is expected, whatever the child experiences as normal in the rest of their lives. There may be tensions enough about how to behave within the school itself, but politicians and at least some educationalists seem to be of the view that it's the school's values and rules that should always dominate, even beyond the gates. This immediately puts up barriers in the minds of some families.

I am not arguing that *all* schools should be more accommodating in the face of such alienation. Most families will fit in with conventional expectations and our education system is probably as good as any in meeting the needs of the overwhelming majority. I am just saying that those on the edge should still be able to find a suitable place somewhere. So often they end up either being excluded altogether, or they choose to exclude themselves, from the one opportunity on offer. Schools all really want the same thing and who can blame them when they have been required to become competitors with each other in a race with only one kind of prize? These families are not at the top of their list of priorities. They never have been.

A culture of blame, or 'naming' and 'shaming' whether it is applied to schools, parents, children or LAs is never going to help. It is good to have targets and measurements of progress, but they can never, in themselves, become the key objective. Children, young people and their families are complicated; some especially so. Solutions are rarely as simple as is sometimes suggested. But keeping them and their needs at the centre must always mean a recognition that this not just about statistics. It's about doing our very best to try and make a difference to the lives of individuals. And we have to keep on trying, not because it always works, but because every single one of them deserves nothing less. Nothing else should be the focus.